# FINANCIAL REPORTING
## in the 1990s
## and BEYOND

1993

a position paper prepared by
Peter H. Knutson, PhD, CPA

Association for
Investment Management
and Research

To obtain an AIMR Publications Catalog or to order additional copies of this publication contact:

AIMR Publications Sales Department
P.O. Box 7947
Charlottesville, Va. 22906
U.S.A.
Telephone: 804/980-3647
Fax: 804/977-0350

*The Association for Investment Management and Research comprises the Institute of Chartered Financial Analysts and the Financial Analysts Federation.*

This publication is designed to provide accurate and authoritative information in regard to the subject matter covered. It is sold with the understanding that the publisher is not engaged in rendering legal, accounting, or other professional service. If legal advice or other expert assistance is required, the services of a competent professional should be sought.

*From a Declaration of Principles jointly adopted by a Committee of the American Bar Association and a Committee of Publishers.*

ISBN 1-879087-30-8

*Printed in the United States of America*

12/15/93

# CONTENTS

# FOREWORD

This report, although authored primarily by one person, represents the collective views of AIMR members: financial analysts, portfolio managers, and other investment professionals. The views of individuals, including those of the author, may differ from the consensus. But that is to be expected. As the report itself makes clear, AIMR members are professionals. As such, they are expected to think for themselves and to draw conclusions on less than complete data. In such circumstances, it is impossible that they would all agree. However, we on the Financial Accounting Policy Committee (FAPC) believe that there are fewer differences among analysts than the charge to the Committee appears to anticipate.

Earlier versions of this publication were circulated for comment to AIMR's constituent societies and to other interested members of the financial community both in the United States and internationally. We received many comments. Those from AIMR societies were considered carefully by the FAPC and incorporated in the final revision as appropriate. Those from others were useful in encouraging us to explain better matters on which there appeared to be misunderstanding or confusion. We also updated certain sections to recognize subsequent events, including the appointment of a practicing financial analyst and CFA to the Financial Accounting Standards Board.

As the principal author of this report, I would like to thank my fellow FAPC members for their support and encouragement throughout the project. The members of the Committee are listed in Appendix C (see page 98). Special thanks are due to Patricia A. McConnell of Bear Stearns & Co., Inc.; Gerald I. White, CFA, of Grace & White, Inc.; and Peter C. Lincoln of the United States Steel and Carnegie Pension Fund. These three individuals served as members of the FAPC subcommittee that oversaw this project and their advice and suggestions were invaluable. Additional thanks go to Raymond J. DeAngelo, former Director of Advocacy for AIMR and now Vice President of Communications and Services, for his thorough reading and constructive comments on each successive draft and to AIMR staff member Rosalie Poss for promptly and accurately responding to all of my several requests for assistance.

Other FAPC members who provided valuable comments and advice on earlier drafts are: Anthony T. Cope, CFA, Wellington Management Company (now with the Financial Accounting Standards Board); Donald H. Korn, CFA, DHK Associates, Inc.; Sharon M. McGarvey, Metropolitan Life Insurance Company; James M. Meyer, CFA, Janney Montgomery Scott, Inc.; Robert L.

Renck, Jr., R.L. Renck & Company, Inc.; Douglas Sherlock, CFA, Sherlock Company; Paul Sloate, Sloate, Weisman, Murray & Company; Ashwinpaul C. Sondhi, Columbia University and New York University; William M. Stellenwerf, Fitch Investor Service, Inc.; and Frances G. Stone, CFA, Merrill, Lynch & Company.

Finally, I am joined by all the members of the FAPC in expressing our appreciation to Mildred M. Hermann, who provided the original inspiration and vision to undertake this project. Ms. Hermann, now retired, was associated with the FAPC in her position as Vice President and Policy Coordinator, first for the Financial Analysts Federation and later for AIMR. The completion of this report is something in which we believe she can take a great deal of pride.

Peter H. Knutson
Member, Financial Accounting Policy Committee
Associate Professor of Accounting
The Wharton School
University of Pennsylvania
*November 1993*

# CHARGE TO THE COMMITTEE

The Financial Accounting Policy Committee is to prepare a report that expresses the views of AIMR members on financial reporting. It should state how and why financial reports are used in the analytic process. It should clearly indicate what disclosures are essential to analysts, not only their format and content, but also the frequency with which they are reported and the means by which they are disseminated. The Committee should define the separate, but complementary, roles of financial analysis and financial reporting.

In its deliberations, the Committee should look to the future. It should appropriately consider the implications of, among others, the following matters:

The rapid globalization of capital markets and the concomitant impact on financial reports, standard setting, and securities market regulation.

The increasing use of electronic means to assemble and examine financial data in quantities previously unaccessible.

The appropriateness of cost-based, industrial-oriented financial reports for growing numbers of financial and other service organizations.

Although the Committee should look primarily to the future, it should not lose continuity with the past. Its deliberations should be extensions of those groups and individuals who produced previous Financial Accounting Policy Committee position papers, and it should draw on their collective wisdom.

The final report of the Committee should take positions and make recommendations on which analysts can agree. In controversial matters where agreement is not apparent, the Committee should present its views together with fair representation of the alternatives. With respect to certain emerging and cutting-edge issues, the Committee's contributions will be (1) to identify the issues and their importance to analysts and (2) to recommend courses of further study.

# EXECUTIVE SUMMARY

"Forces now at work are likely to have an impact on the nature and extent of financial reporting in this decade and beyond." Those words were used during the February 3, 1992, meeting of the AIMR Board of Governors that authorized the preparation of the this report.

It was written to promulgate and disseminate AIMR viewpoints on substantially all matters relating to the interrelationship between financial analysis and financial reporting and disclosure. This summary conveys only the most essential topics and points made therein, and the Financial Accounting Policy Committee (FAPC) commends the full report to all readers.

## Financial Analysis and Financial Reporting

This section provides primarily descriptive information. It discusses the interrelationship between the efficient market hypothesis and other theories of financial economics and the role of financial analysis in making markets efficient. It presents a description of the analytic process to the extent that generalizations can be made in that area. It lists and describes the vast variety of information sources used by analysts, of which financial reports are an indispensable part of the whole. It then describes in more detail each of the financial reports analysts rely on in their work.

One of the most important functions of this section is to define the distinction between financial analysis and financial reporting. The committee believes that financial reporting should be concerned with presenting the economic history of specific economic entities and that it is best done when managements also are willing to disclose and discuss their strategies, proposed tactics and plans, and expected outcomes. Forecasts of the future and similar material enhance financial report usefulness, but these must be separated from and not confused with the financial statements themselves. The function of analysis is to allow those who participate in the financial markets to form their own rational expectations about future economic events, in particular the amounts, timing, and uncertainty of an enterprise's future cash flows. Through that process, analysts form opinions about the absolute and relative value of individual companies, make investment decisions or cause them to be made, and thereby contribute to the economically efficient allocation of capital and clearing of the capital markets.

## The Changing World and Its Implications for Analysis

The world constantly is changing, and everyone must adjust to accommodate those forces over which they have no control. The nature and implications of three major phenomena that are expected to affect financial analysis and analysts are considered here. Those matters also have considerable influence on the views and conclusions expressed later in this report.

First, globalization of the capital markets and the spread of free enterprise throughout the world have enormous implications for analysts. Capital flows freely across many national borders. The need for information to compare investment opportunities of disparate character is greater than ever. Thus, an increasing amount of attention has been given to the activities of the International Accounting Standards Committee and the International Organization of Securities Commissioners. We express our support for continued advancement of their work, but we also express concern over the possible lowering of standards of accounting, disclosure, reporting frequency, and attestation. In sum, because rapid internationalization serves the interests of financial analysts, we support it—but only if it is done so as to raise the level of information internationally without lowering it domestically.

Second, the accessibility of computing power continues to rise as rapidly as its cost falls, which has several implications for financial analysis. Quantitative analysis becomes practicable to an extent never dreamed of previously. There are more and ever-increasing demands for and uses of data bases of financial information. We look forward to the general availability of the SEC's Electronic Data Gathering And Retrieval system. All this means that financial analysis will require more emphasis than ever before on recognition and measurement in financial reports so that we may be assured that the contents of data bases are both complete and comparable.

Third, the accounting model used today was developed to fit enterprises whose economic activity is primarily in manufacturing or merchandising. Today, services of all types constitute a major portion of economic endeavors. Financial assets play a larger role as more funds are saved and invested than ever before. The current accounting model has been challenged on many fronts. Our conclusion is that although we consider it fundamentally sound, there are nevertheless many ways in which it could be employed more efficaciously than it is today. Much of the remainder of this report is devoted to describing our suggestions for improvement.

## Qualitative Characteristics of Financial Statements

The qualitative characteristics of accounting that we find most important to the needs of financial analysts are relevance, reliability (both verifiability and representational faithfulness), timeliness, and neutrality. First, analysts need to know economic reality—what is really going on—to the greatest extent it can be depicted by accounting numbers. The information must be relevant to the process of analysis, one reason why much space in the early part of this report is devoted to describing the analyst's work.

Some attention is paid in this section to the need for timely reporting. It introduces the view of AIMR that mandated quarterly reporting not only is essential, but also that moves to abolish it appear to be based on incorrect premises; in other words, it is inappropriate to blame quarterly reporting requirements for "short-termism" when the blame can better be placed elsewhere.

## Broad Topics of Current Importance to Analysts

The largest part of the report is devoted to the broad subjects that follow, and each of them is discussed in considerable depth. The brief summaries here indicate only the scope of that coverage and list the major recommendations that result.

**Mark-to-Market Accounting.** Value versus Valuation. Any imminent change to mark-to-market accounting is not welcomed by the majority of financial analysts. Many would not be happy to see historic costs removed from the financial statements, and these analysts are not convinced that there would be an increase in relevance sufficient to offset the reduction in reliability of the new data. Others disagree and are anxious to see and use market values in their work. In fact, the spectrum of opinion among analysts on the subject is so broad that it cannot be represented succinctly here; additional study of the issues by a subcommittee of the FAPC has been initiated. Furthermore, analyst opinion varies depending on the extent to which mark-to-market accounting would apply. Some would approve of it for financial instruments or some financial instruments but not for tangible or other intangible assets. There is agreement, at least within the FAPC, that marketable equity securities should be reported at market and that the disclosures of market values of financial instruments required by Financial Accounting Standard No. 107 will provide useful information without any corresponding loss of other data.

**Accounting for Intangible Assets.** Contemporary accounting for intangible assets has great potential for confusion. Purchased intangibles are initially recorded at cost and amortized over periods of time that often are arbitrarily determined. Self-developed intangibles are for the most part not recorded. Financial statement comparability between and among enterprises suffers accordingly. Our contemplation of this situation leads us to two major recommendations that we believe will increase comparability. Both recommendations are controversial and should be considered in the light of the full discussion of them in this report.

First, we advocate capitalization of all executory contracts with an initial duration of more than one year. We would include not only leases but also employment agreements and similar contractual arrangements. Our recommendation does not advocate any change that would weaken the standards governing revenue recognition.

Second, we recommend that purchased goodwill be written off at the date it is acquired. We believe that it is an important number, but only to depict a value at a particular date—a value that undoubtedly is subject to rapid and sizable potential change thereafter. We cannot see how its presence on the balance sheet is of use in estimating a firm's future cash flows or gauging its contemporaneous value. Therefore, we recommend banishing goodwill from an enterprise's list of assets, but preserving a record of it by having it show as a separate and distinct reduction of shareholders' equity.

**Financial Statement Dissemination.** In recent years, mandated quarterly reporting in the United States has come under increasing attack. Many charges have been leveled, most recently that it leads to "short-termism" and that it causes the U.S. to lack competitiveness with the rest of the world (where most reports are issued only semi-annually). We feel strongly that these charges are wrong, and this section provides an exposition of the virtues of quarterly reporting, refutation of the arguments against it, and an initial argument for disaggregated quarterly information.

Obviously, financial markets and financial analysis thrive on information. Furthermore, information will eventually find its way to influence market prices, whether the avenues it takes are legitimate or not. As investment professionals who take pride in our ethical conduct, we need to have information that is frequent, reliable, and relevant. We need to have it disseminated even-handedly so that it becomes available to all market participants at the same time, rather than first to the privileged few. We believe the arguments against quarterly reporting are specious, and we give substantial reasons to support that opinion.

**Disaggregated Financial Statements.**  Analysis of a complex economic entity requires information about the workings of each of its components. There is no disagreement among AIMR members that segment information is totally vital to their work.  There also is general agreement among them that the current segment reporting standard, Financial Accounting Standard No. 14, is inadequate. Recent work by a subcommittee of the FAPC has confirmed that a substantial majority of analysts seek and, when it is available, use quarterly segment data.

The Financial Accounting Standards Board (FASB) has in process a project on disaggregation for which AIMR provided partial financial support in addition to its overall endorsement.  We do not wish to prejudge the results of a project now in its initial stages, but we do suggest an avenue for the FASB to explore.  We believe that segment data are most useful when they depict the way in which the enterprise itself is organized and managed, and we urge the FASB to seek ways to promulgate a standard that produces such a result, despite the several difficulties in doing so that we acknowledge and discuss in this report.

**Income and Cash Flow Statements.**  Throughout the report, there are repeated recommendations that the FASB needs to develop its concept of "comprehensive income."  Much of this section of the report is devoted to integrating those references and explaining in much greater detail all the reasons why that development is needed—and how the FASB should proceed.

The other part of this section deals with the cash flow statement.  Most AIMR members were pleased with the issuance of Financial Accounting Standard No. 95, which requires that a cash flow statement replace the less-useful statement of changes in financial position.  Most are not pleased with the quality of information contained in many of the cash flow statements they currently receive.  First, virtually no companies have chosen to present cash flows from operations on the direct method.  Failure to do so has been accompanied by arguments that are unconvincing because they are contradictory.  Second, because so many cash flow statements contain detectable errors, we call for establishment of an authoritative literature on cash flow statement preparation.

**Transition to New Standards.**  Financial analysts support the issuance of accounting standards that improve the quality and quantity of financial information.  The antithesis is that any new standard disrupts or destroys time-series analysis by making future periods' financial reports not comparable to those of the past. We have observed a trend towards exacerbation of that situation in the transition methods permitted by the FASB in several recent standards.

First, there are delayed final adoption dates, thus permitting extended periods of noncomparability between the financial statements of early adopters and those of companies that wait until the final date to adopt. Second, there are choices of method—restatement, cumulative effect, or (worst of all) delayed effect. In the case of Financial Accounting Standard No. 106, it will be 20 years after the final adoption date before we begin to have total comparability among enterprises. In the meantime, it will take an astute and fortuitous reading of complex footnotes by the analyst to ferret out the truth. In this section, we recommend single transition methods and short transition periods.

**The Standard-Setting Process.** Several topics are covered in this section. First is our assertion of support for the continued development of globally acceptable accounting standards. That support is accompanied by a discussion of the problems that we expect will be encountered in the quest for worldwide standards. Second, we express our support for the standard-setting process in the United States and for the FASB as an institution. We provide refutation to many of the criticisms directed against it. We do not believe the FASB is to blame for many of the complications in financial statements today, nor do we believe that it has issued too many standards too quickly. We disagree with those who say its standards are too theoretical, that the cost of implementing them is too great, or that the FASB is inimical to the interests of financial statement preparers. Rather than following due process too little, we believe the FASB follows it too much. The reasons supporting these beliefs are set forth in this report.

Finally, we emphasize the needs of financial statement users in the standards-setting process. We argue that users of financial statements are also the owners of the enterprises being reported upon, and it is the users who, in addition to receiving the benefits, ultimately bear the cost of providing financial reports. We suggest that user viewpoints be incorporated in the standard-setting process through their direct participation as members of the FASB, in addition to the current practice of users providing written comments and oral testimony.

## Summary of Important Positions and Guide to Future Actions

Many recommendations are made throughout this report in the context of individual topic discussions. Those singled out for special emphasis at the end of the report are these:

1. Strive for globally acceptable accounting principles, including disclosure standards.
2. Set financial information in its business context.
3. Continue to deliberate the role of current values in financial reports.
4. Recognize all executory contracts.
5. Develop standards for reporting comprehensive income.
6. Provide frequent and detailed financial reports.
7. Consider cost/benefit analysis from a user viewpoint.

## Conclusions

Throughout the report, we make many other recommendations and establish positions on a variety of issues. Those matters are set forth for two purposes. First, they announce to the rest of the world our thoughts on issues of mutual importance to investment professionals and to other constituents in the world of financial reporting. Second, they provide an opportunity for AIMR members themselves to form their individual thoughts about the implications of financial reporting and its potential effect on their work in the 1990s and beyond.

# PREFACE

The Association for Investment Management and Research (AIMR) was formed through a merger of the Institute of Chartered Financial Analysts, founded in 1962, and the Financial Analysts Federation, founded in 1947. Its mission is stated in its name—to advance the art and science of investment management and research. This is accomplished through programs and other activities that include the CFA candidate program, advocacy, continuing education, ethics and professional standards, and public awareness. AIMR also recognizes through awards distinguished service and accomplishments by individual investment professionals.

## AIMR Membership

AIMR members are investment management professionals. Membership includes securities analysts, portfolio managers, strategists, consultants, and other investment specialists. Members practice in fields such as investment counseling and management, banking, insurance, investment banking, and brokerage. Of AIMR's more than 24,000 members, some 64 percent hold the designation Chartered Financial Analyst in recognition of passing three sequential CFA examinations. Roughly 70 percent of AIMR members hold degrees beyond the baccalaureate; 86 percent are located in the United States, with 10 percent living in Canada and the remainder in other countries.

Investment management professionals often are categorized by activity into what are called "buy-side" analysts and "sell-side" analysts. The latter are likely to be employed in the research departments of investment banking and brokerage firms. Their reports tend to focus on individual companies; in larger firms, they specialize by industry. The work of buy-side analysts is less often seen because it is usually produced for confidential use by the analyst's employer, more often than not a portfolio manager or investment counselor.

In addition to being employed in the broadly defined securities industry, AIMR members also engage in an impressive range of other employments. There are many analysts employed by business and consulting firms that are engaged in competitive analysis, the appraisal of competitors within their industry, and analysis of potential acquisitions. There are analyst specialists, such as those who concentrate on accounting issues or other technical support areas within a financial firm's research department. A small number of AIMR members are academics.

A recent survey by AIMR's Financial Accounting Policy Committee (FAPC) showed that virtually all of these investment professionals use financial reports in their work either directly or indirectly. Several of them utilize financial information accumulated in and accessed through data bases. At the other extreme, many of them read volumes of financial statements in complete detail. Others fall in between and may combine using data bases with reading financial reports in detail on a selective basis.

## Advocacy by AIMR

The function of advocacy has as its goal to support fair treatment for investors and to encourage high ethical and professional standards in the investment industry. It encompasses such diverse, but not unrelated, topics as bondholder rights, government relations, performance presentation standards, and proxy voting rights. Many of AIMR's advocacy efforts are expended in the realm of financial reporting and corporate information. The AIMR Corporate Information Committee each year publishes a report that evaluates the quality of corporate financial reporting in selected industries and makes awards for excellence.

The FAPC maintains contact with both private and public sector accounting groups that establish accounting standards to ensure that the needs of investors are communicated and included as standards are promulgated. (A list of written comments for the past six years, 1988–93, by the FAPC to various standard-setting and regulatory bodies is included in this report as Appendix A.) In addition to written comments, FAPC members also provide testimony to the Financial Accounting Standards Board (FASB) as appropriate; the FAPC as a whole meets with the FASB annually and from time to time with SEC officials. The Financial Accounting Standards Advisory Council usually includes one FAPC member. The current FAPC chairman is a member of the Board of the International Accounting Standards Committee, and an FAPC member was recently appointed to the FASB.

## Purpose and Content of This Report

From time to time, the FAPC has issued broad position papers on accounting and financial reporting. The first of these papers, dated March 30, 1972, was addressed to the American Institute of Certified Public Accountants (AICPA) Accounting Objectives Study Group, known informally as the Trueblood

Commission. Subsequent papers—dated September 15, 1974; July 22, 1977; March 14, 1978; and March 31, 1978—were addressed to the FASB as it was formulating and setting in motion its conceptual framework project. The current report continues the tradition of occasional position papers by the FAPC. As such, it presents the views of the largest and most important organized group of financial statement users in our economy and in the world. An earlier version received wide circulation and comment from AIMR member societies and others. Those comments have been incorporated in this report.

It also is important from time to time for the FAPC to take positions that are proactive. Much of its work (see Appendix A) consists of responding to initiatives of various groups including accounting standard-setting bodies, the FASB and the IASC; capital markets regulators such as the SEC and its Office of the Chief Accountant; organizations representing financial statement preparers, such as the Financial Executives' Institute (FEI) and others; and auditors, such as the AICPA, the Canadian Institute of Chartered Accountants, and similar organizations in other countries. For the FAPC to be more consistent and productive in its written and oral communications with those groups, it needs to consider its own positions on current and impending issues relating to financial reporting. Even more important, it must ponder the implications of recent and anticipated changes in the environment in which the securities industry does business.

Since the 1970s, there have been many changes in the financial world and in financial reporting. The FASB has evolved from an institution in its formative stages, defining itself and its agenda, to a mature organization that receives criticism as well as praise for its work. Regulation of financial reporting by the SEC and other governmental bodies has not remained unaffected by the political currents and ideologies that govern Washington and Ottawa. Additionally, the SEC is in the initial stages of instituting its Electronic Data Gathering And Retrieval system, which will change many of the basic rules of how financial data are disseminated. Financial markets have become globalized to an extent not contemplated in the 1970s, with extensions forthcoming as the political economies of eastern Europe transform themselves.

The world is a far different place than it was only a few years ago, and it has evolved in ways that only a visionary could have predicted. Thus, it is hazardous to conjecture now about what the future will bring. But the business of financial analysis and securities analysts is to form rational expectations about future events. So it is with some experience in pondering the future that AIMR's FAPC turns its attention in this report to financial reporting issues that it believes are and will be significant during the 1990s and beyond.

## Reasons for Reporting At This Time

In recent months, both the AICPA and the FEI—the groups representing, respectively, the main bodies of auditors and preparers of financial statements—have begun work on major projects to study financial reporting. In 1991, the Financial Accounting Foundation, the parent and sponsor of the FASB, formed an oversight committee of its board of directors to evaluate the operations and product of the FASB. Thus, in the financial reporting milieu, the standard-setting body, preparers of financial statements, and auditors all are in the process of presenting their views to the world. AIMR, as the primary organization representing financial statement users, needs to be heard at least as clearly and resoundingly as other groups involved with financial reporting.

In the past, FAPC position papers have been addressed to groups responsible in some way for establishing accounting standards. This report seeks a broader audience. Its primary purpose is to influence the opinions and actions of (1) the managements of the companies that prepare and issue financial reports, (2) the accounting standard setters and securities markets regulators who set the parameters within which those reports must fall, and (3) the independent auditors who attest to the fairness of those reports. The overriding message to each of those groups is that the purpose of external financial reporting is to serve the needs of those who use it.

This report also is one of the initial major policy initiatives since the formation of AIMR. Previous works of its predecessor bodies represented the views of their separate constituencies. Now, we have the opportunity to produce what we hope is the first of a series of policy statements and reports that will present the collective views all AIMR members, securities analysts, and other investment professionals.

# FINANCIAL ANALYSIS AND FINANCIAL REPORTING

## The Nature and Role of Efficient Markets

During the past 25 years or so, a great literature has been created that supports the hypothesis that financial markets are, to one degree or another, efficient. *How* efficient is a matter of debate among both practitioners and academics even today. In its most basic form, the efficient market hypothesis (EMH) states that information is quickly impounded in stock prices. The implications are that one cannot profit by having access to information that also is available to others. The evidence supporting the EMH is voluminous in the literatures of economics, finance, and accounting. There also is abundant literature that points out anomalies in the EMH. The degree to which market efficiency actually exists is a matter that will continue to be debated for some time to come.

What we all may agree upon is that information does affect stock prices eventually. The corollary is that markets could not possibly be efficient if information were not available. In addition, those who either lack information or who do not understand the information that is available to all are at a distinct disadvantage in buying or selling securities. Therefore, no matter how efficient or inefficient a financial market may be, information is its lifeblood.

Financial information comes from many sources and in many forms. Much of it is received by financial analysts prior to the issuance of financial reports. The news wires are filled with items giving information about major events affecting various companies: new contracts, new financing, legal actions, product introductions, patent grants, capital spending plans, personnel changes, and the like. Companies send out press releases, hold analyst meetings, and otherwise see that news affecting them is presented in the most favorable light. Much of the information that moves the market is qualitative in nature and requires subsequent verification. It is used by analysts to form estimates of future earnings and cash flows and to draw conclusions about whether a particular company's securities should be bought, held, or sold.

Financial statements and other formal financial reports are usually produced some time after the fact. They provide analysts the assurance that their initial interpretations of company news were sensible and to some degree accurate. Sometimes it is asserted that financial statements do not contain new information. Analysts hope that assertion is true. If it is, that means that both the companies and the analysts who follow them have done their jobs successfully in making the market as efficient as can be. When a financial statement contains a "surprise" or two that causes a market price to change, one usually may conclude either that the analyst lacked perspicacity or that the company engaged in duplicity.

Although a financial report may not contain "news," that does not mean that it does not contain information. Later in this report, we point out the many ways in which such reports provide not only a record of the past, but also clues to the future and a myriad of detailed data not available elsewhere. The overriding mission of this report is to discuss in detail exactly how that information should be presented so as to be of optimal use to financial analysts and, in turn, the efficiency of capital markets.

## Analysts Look for Anomalies Between Price and Value

The function of markets is to set prices and effect transactions. The function of financial analysis is to assess values. If markets were truly efficient, price would adjust quickly to value as information became available and its implications were understood. Even in the most efficient of markets, however, different people assess value differently. The dividend discount model (DDM) valuation framework is often used to estimate the worth of a security as the present value of its future dividends plus its residual price discounted at a risk-adjusted rate of return. The capital asset pricing model provides an analytical framework to relate expected return and risk. But tolerance of risk varies among individuals, as do estimates of the amounts, timing, and uncertainty of future dividends. A market price is at the margin: Persons who continue to hold securities believe them to be worth at least their market price and to be appropriate to the portfolio.

Financial analysts look for market price anomalies, securities whose values are perceived to be different from their current market prices—usually greater but sometimes less. In doing so, analysts form projections of future earnings, usually as a surrogate for estimating future cash flows. Major events in the economic life of a company may cause analysts to reassess the company's future earnings and may in turn be reflected through significant changes in the market price of the company's securities. Analysts' reports are used by securities firms to make buy, sell, or hold recommendations. Portfolio managers and other investors actually make buy-sell-hold decisions. As investors change their minds about the values of individual securities, they change their portfolios accordingly. Thus, capital is allocated efficiently and impersonally to its best use in the economy.

Financial analysts also participate in due diligence proceedings, advising deal makers and investors as to the economic values underlying proposed transactions. Other analysts prepare valuation studies to assess competition and competitors. Others are consultants on valuation. In sum, if markets are efficient, they are made so by the work of financial analysts who continually are seeking to find discrepancies between price and value and who advise on portfolio transactions accordingly. This moves market prices toward price–value equilibrium.

## Sources of Information

A common starting point in the analytic process is to assess the state of the economy and the various industries within it. Information to do so comes from a variety of sources.

**Economic and Industry Reports.** Economic reports and prognoses are available both from the government and from private sources. Many financial firms have their own in-house economic experts who provide continual updating to the rest of the firm, its customers, and sometimes to outsiders.

Industry-specific data come from the government, trade associations, the business press, and a variety of other sources. Often they are obtained indirectly from companies within the industry. Analysts who follow a particular industry usually participate in meetings, conventions, trade shows, and other industry-wide events. They also must keep up to date on technological advances and other industry changes.

**Company-Specific Information.**[1] Financial reports are the beginning and ending points in obtaining information about individual companies. As a starter, they provide an overview of the company's business, its status, and its performance for a series of years. It is difficult to think of a better primer than the combination of an annual report to shareholders (complete with the chairman's letter to shareholders, financial statements, management's discussion and analysis, and other descriptive material) and a Form 10-K (with all of its detailed description of business, facilities, risks, contingencies, and other mandated disclosures). At the end of the information gathering process, financial reports are used to corroborate the vast array of company-specific

---

[1]For a more detailed report on financial analyst sources of company-specific information, particularly in connection with analysts' interface with the investor relations activities of publicly owned firms, see "Securities Analysts, Investment Managers, and Corporate Issuers of Securities" (Washington, D.C.: National Investor Relations Institute, forthcoming).

data assembled from the various sources described next.

Many of the data used by analysts come directly from companies themselves. Sources include press releases and other announcements, including preliminary earnings numbers. Information is received orally from company executives, sometimes in analysts' meetings, other times by telephone or during analysts' visits to the company's premises. Plant visits and field trips allow analysts to compare the company's written and oral representations to the reality of its operating conditions and atmosphere. Many companies entertain analysts, usually in groups, so that the companies may present their stories in the most favorable circumstances. One of the tasks of an analyst is to sort through all of the favorable information to discover and weigh the facts that are most germane to assessing a company's future prospects.

The business press provides substantial amounts of information about individual companies, much of which is now captured in data bases. In some instances, a clipping service may be used to gather data on a particular company. Almost every major industry and many subdivisions of them are covered by specialized publications. These are "must reading" for industry specialist analysts who use them to gather intelligence, not only about the state of the industry, but also about the performance and status of the individual firms it comprises.

Finally, a great deal of information about individual companies may be obtained through government documents and filings. One example is the call reports filed with the U.S. Comptroller of the Currency by banks. Another is the filings by insurance companies, public utilities, and other regulated companies with state and federal commissions. Individual company pension plan filings with the United States Department of Labor are another example. U.S. General Accounting Office studies, and public hearings conducted by Congressional committees and regulatory agencies are other important sources of information. Under some circumstances, shareholders holding as little as 1 percent of a company's shares may obtain copies of its federal income tax returns. Since enactment of the Freedom of Information Act, more specific company data have been available to the public. In a number of cases, however, the incremental value of the available data may be less than the cost of the effort necessary to obtain it.

## Financial Reports Used By Analysts

The use of financial reports will differ from analyst to analyst, depending on the purpose of the analysis and the analyst's personal style. In fact, there even is a minuscule number of analysts who assert that they do not use financial reports in their work.[2] The depth of an analyst's study of financial reports is in inverse proportion to the number of companies he or she follows. To some extent, that depth also is a function of the analyst's interest in and understanding of financial accounting and reporting standards and disclosures.

At the top of every analyst's list is the annual report to shareholders. It is the major reporting document, and every other financial report is in some respect subsidiary or supplementary to it. That is one of the reasons AIMR and its predecessor organizations have consistently opposed companies issuing what is called a "summary annual report." Financial analysts expect the annual report to shareholders to contain a complete set of financial statements. Even though, for such companies, a full set of audited financial statements must be included in the proxy statement, it may not be received routinely by a non-shareholder analyst. Furthermore, the financial statements contained in a "summary annual report" are incomplete and may well mislead less sophisticated investors who are unaware of that fact.

The annual report on Form 10-K is regarded by most analysts as an essential complement to the annual report. It contains several important types of supplementary financial schedules. In addition, it provides detailed descriptions of the business and contains a record, available nowhere else, of other available documents incorporated by reference.

Other than the financial statements themselves, perhaps the most useful single part of the annual report is the management discussion and analysis (MD&A) mandated for inclusion by the SEC. Its information content varies from company to company, but it provides for all companies insights that are not apparent from the financial statements alone. It discloses items that tend to make year-to-year income numbers noncomparable. It provides narratives to accompany the factual disclosures in financial statement notes. It has been less effective in giving management the opportunity to discuss the company's plans and prospects, information that is of utmost relevance to analysts. Although the MD&A is less than perfect, we have detected progressive improvements over time, many of which can be attributed to the efforts of the SEC to enhance its quality.

Analysts are constantly updating their projections and need timely financial reports to assess how well they and the companies they follow are doing. Quarterly reports are vital to the analytic process, particularly the detailed

---

[2]These are more likely than not to be cases in which the analyst has delegated actual financial report reading and analysis to one or more subordinates.

reports provided on SEC Form 10-Q, which include a mandated MD&A section. Many analysts also find helpful the management representations contained in the briefer quarterly reports to shareholders. For reasons set forth in detail later in this report, we oppose the movement in certain quarters to eliminate or otherwise attenuate interim financial reporting.

Many companies publish and distribute on request additional financial and statistical information beyond that contained in their annual reports. These "fact books" or similar documents are used extensively by analysts. The proxy statement provides information about compensation of the company's senior management and the shareholdings of directors and officers. Form 8-K gives information on major current developments affecting the company. There also are a variety of special financial reports that are peculiar to particular industries and/or companies that analysts find useful in their work.

## Distinguishing Financial Analysis from Financial Reporting

It is quite easy to make a conceptual distinction between financial reporting and financial analysis. Although both result in expressions of worth or value, their perspectives are diametrically opposed. Financial statements express net worth as the surplus of total assets over total liabilities. Because assets and liabilities are both the result of *past* transactions and events[3], so is the accounting measure of net worth. Financial analysis, on the other hand, assesses, estimates, and gauges value solely in terms of expectations of the *future*. A standard concept of value is that embodied in the DDM, which postulates the value of a security to be the present value of its expected future dividends plus its estimated residual price at some specified future date, discounted at a risk-adjusted rate of return (opportunity cost of capital). Thus financial analysts seek to prognosticate the amounts, timing, and risk attached to a firm's future cash flows—either directly or through such surrogates as earnings forecasts.

Statement of Financial Accounting Concepts No. 1, "Objectives of Financial Reporting by Business Enterprises," states in paragraph 37,

---

[3]Statement of Financial Accounting Concepts No. 6 defines assets as "... probable future economic benefits obtained or controlled by a particular entity as the result of *past* transactions or events" (paragraph 25, emphasis added). "Liabilities are probable future sacrifices of economic benefits arising from present obligations of a particular entity to transfer assets or provide services to other entities in the future as a result of *past* transactions or events" (paragraph 35, emphasis added).

> Financial reporting should provide information to help present and potential investors and creditors and other users in assessing the amounts, timing and uncertainty of prospective cash receipts from dividends or interest and the proceeds from the sale, redemption or maturity of securities or loans. The prospects for those cash receipts are affected by the enterprise's ability to generate enough cash to meet its obligations when due and its other cash operating needs, to reinvest in operations, and to pay cash dividends and may also be affected by perceptions of investors and creditors generally about that ability, which affect market prices of the enterprise's securities. Thus, financial reporting should provide information to help investors, creditors, and others assess the amounts, timing, and uncertainty of prospective cash flows to the related enterprise.

A footnote to paragraph 37 explains that the objective "neither requires nor prohibits 'cash flow information,' 'current value information,' 'management forecast information,' or any other specific information." Statement of Financial Accounting Concepts No. 5, "Recognition and Measurement in Financial Statements of Business Enterprises" (FAC 5) on page 5, limits measurement in accounting to the financial statements themselves.

The question then arises regarding the proper relationships among (1) financial statements, (2) notes to financial statements, supplementary information, and other means of financial reporting, and (3) financial analysis, which according to FAC 5 falls outside of financial reporting. To what extent should assessment of the amounts, timing, and uncertainty of an enterprise's future cash flows fall into each of those three categories?

We believe that financial reporting should be concerned with presenting the economic history of specific economic entities and that it is best done when managements also are willing to disclose and discuss their strategies, proposed tactics and plans, and expected outcomes. It is self-evident that reporting on the past always requires the use of estimates and other assessments of future events: uncollectible receivables, depreciable lives, warranty repair costs, and the like. Forecasts of the future and similar material enhances financial report usefulness, but they must be separated from and not confused with the financial statements themselves. Financial analysts avidly seek management's forecasts as part of the financial reporting process, accompanying but not incorporated in the financial statements.

Financial analysts, in turn, must digest all relevant economic information that can affect an economic entity, including but not limited to its financial reports. The function of analysis is to allow those who participate in the financial markets to form their own rational expectations about future economic events, in particular the amounts, timing, and uncertainty of an enterprise's future cash flows. Through this process, analysts form opinions about the absolute and relative value of individual companies, make investment decisions or cause them to be made, and thereby contribute to the economically efficient allocation of capital and clearing of the capital markets. Allocation decisions are made primarily on the basis of comparisons. Financial reporting and financial analysis cross paths because, ultimately, economic value (wealth) is created by expectations of future inflows of economic benefits, primarily in the form of or the equivalent of cash flows. The amounts and timing of future cash flows are in most cases uncertain to various degrees. It is the function of analysis to deal rationally with that uncertainty. It is the function of financial reporting to provide data useful to analysts making assessments of an enterprise's future cash flows and its value today. Such data include detailed and up-to-date information on the amounts and timing of past cash flows, periodic wealth increases from operating activities (profitability), economic status at regular past intervals, and an abundance of supplementary data necessary to understand their content and significance.

Some persons may confuse the roles of financial reporting and financial analysis because of the function of forward-looking information, which is essentially of two different types. First are amounts that we expect to see reported in financial statements and subject to audit: receivables, payables, a variety of financial instruments reported at the present value of their future cash flows. These are contractually determined amounts arising from past exchanges that meet the definitions of assets or liabilities, even though their value is properly determined by the amounts of related future exchanges. The other type of forward-looking information comprises forecasts, projections, and certain pro-forma presentations. These numbers are of great importance and usefulness to analysts, but they are not part of the economic history of the firm and therefore not proper financial statement components. Nor are they auditable, although the participation of an independent accountant in their preparation could well enhance their credibility and "user-friendliness" as well as provide some assurance that management's methodology was sound, its assumptions reasonable, and its calculations accurate.

## How Financial Reporting Can Serve Financial Analysis

The starting point in analysis of a specific company is to look at the record.

How has that management and company performed in the past, and what is its status at present? Answers to those questions are found in the company's financial statements. Past performance is evaluated in terms of profitability and liquidity, current status in terms of financial position. Financial statements are valuable to the extent that they provide useful and comprehensive information that allow financial analysts to evaluate how well management has done with the resources at its command. Although the word "stewardship" no longer is fashionable, it fits here. In fact, it continues to be a major reason for the accounting profession to continue producing financial statements in their traditional format.

The specific content of financial statements is discussed in more detail in other sections of this report, but it is important here to state how essential it is that financial reports be comprehensive. If we are to have financial statements in the traditional form, they ought to include what they purport to contain. For example, many so-called "off balance sheet" items should be on the balance sheet. Another matter on which FAPC members are agreed is the urgent need for the FASB to develop, in the form of financial accounting standards, the notion of "comprehensive income" that it introduced in Financial Accounting Concepts Nos. 3 and 6. If done properly, such standards would bring back to a structured income statement various items that now bypass income on their way to the owners' equity section of the balance sheet. The topic of comprehensive income is discussed at greater length later in this report.

Analysts need financial statements structured so as to be consistent with how the business is organized and managed. That means that two different companies in the same industry may have to report segment data differently because they are structured differently themselves. Perhaps one may be organized by product line, the other by geographical area or by the types of industries represented by its customers. There are even more possibilities of organizational differences between and among companies in different industries. Some may be production oriented, others driven by markets or research activity. We also are aware of the difficulty of setting accounting and disclosure standards to meet our needs, and our more detailed topical discussions later in this report incorporate that concern.

Financial reports have to be understandable. Analysts are quite aware of the technically demanding nature of certain accounting standards and we sympathize with financial statement preparers and their auditors for the additional work they must do. These standards were promulgated, however, because they are intended to provide vital economic information to investors, creditors, and other financial statement users. We worry that the purpose of a standard can be thwarted by a grudging compliance with only its technical requirements. We look in financial reports for information—and often its provision requires explanations that go beyond the minimum reporting requirements contained in a standard or checklist.

The financial reporting process is most useful when it goes beyond the past and present to include management's views of its future strategies, plans, and expectations. For example, management currently is required in the MD&A section of its annual report to shareholders to report how the results of each of the past three years differ one from another. The SEC strongly encourages but does not require similar discussion of how management expects the results of future years to differ from those of the past. Why have managements been so slow to respond to this urging? We have seen some improvement recently, but the pace is glacial.

Financial reports also should provide assurance that the organization is under control. At one extreme, this means that it conducts its affairs at least lawfully and conforms to the ethical norms of the jurisdictions and cultures in which it operates. In another sense, we seek assurance that the company is being operated in the interests of its shareholders and creditors for its stated purposes and with the goal of maximizing wealth in a responsible manner. Analysts also need a depiction of what the enterprise is doing in the areas of social and environmental impact as well as assurance that control systems to ensure compliance are in place and operative. We believe this is an area for expanded disclosure.

# THE CHANGING WORLD AND
# ITS IMPLICATIONS FOR ANALYSIS

## Globalization and the Spread of Free Enterprise

Recent decades have seen an astonishing disappearance of geographical barriers both physical and psychological. Markets for products have become international; no longer do we think of the United States alone when we speak of market share in automobiles, electronic equipment, computers, and a variety of other industrial and consumer goods.

Financial markets have not escaped this phenomenon. Large companies raise money throughout the world, in forms and locations that offer the most favorable terms. Investors follow suit by making capital available for equity investing around the globe.

Globalization of the capital markets will likely continue until such time as almost all barriers have disappeared. During 1993, the European Community is scheduled to spring into full-blown being. Intra-European economic barriers between individual members of the community are going down rapidly, although not without certain difficulties, and other non-member European countries are waiting to be admitted. Even Switzerland, that bastion of autonomous independence, appears ready to join. The collapse of communistic socialism in Eastern Europe has implications not only for those countries but also for certain other countries that emulated them.

All of this change and its projected continuance have dramatic implications for financial analysis, many of which go beyond the limited scope of this report. They are caused by differences in languages and cultures, laws and ethics, business practices, and financial institutions and instruments. With respect to financial reporting alone, there are a myriad of problems to consider. These encompass analysts' needs for internationally acceptable standards of financial reporting—including common accounting methods, adequate detailed disclosure, sufficient frequency of reporting, and credible auditing or other reliability enhancement.

**Common Accounting Methods.** The International Accounting Standards Committee (IASC) has done an admirable job with meager resources in bringing together accounting and standards-setting bodies from around the world to deal with the accounting standards problem. It has had two major accomplishments to date. First, it has codified accounting practice around the world (deeming idiosyncratic methods unacceptable and allowing to stand alternative methods that were followed in sizable portions of the world). Its second accomplishment is its "Improvements Project" to eliminate many remaining alternatives in practice while at the same time initiating new projects (such as joint venture accounting and financial instruments) on which few national standards currently exist.

We applaud the IASC for its productivity. But we also must look carefully at factors that may impair its ongoing effectiveness. First, it now is entering politically precarious territory and is without the power of an SEC to back it up. Although its work is supported by the International Organization of Securities Commissions (IOSCO), its authority is limited, as is that of the IASC itself, to the willingness of sovereign governments to be persuaded to adopt its views. Second, the politics of international standard setting may be exacerbated because the IASC is composed primarily of representatives of national professional accounting bodies, such as the American Institute of Certified Public Accountants (AICPA) in the United States, rather than being an amalgamation of national standard-setting bodies. Third, in the United States and Canada, it is the Financial Accounting Standards Board (FASB) and the Canadian Institute of Chartered Accountants, respectively, that are designated to determine accounting standards. Under the FASB's rules of due process, it is almost impossible for it to participate directly in international standards setting, but it has reorganized its internal procedures to take account of international developments and sends an observer to all meetings of the IASC board.

**Adequate Detailed Disclosure.** This is an adjunct to the problem of common accounting standards. It raises the question of the extent to which an enterprise's securities can be issued and traded in a foreign country while adhering only to the disclosure standards of its home country. This is a current issue involving movement on the part of the SEC and its counterparts in the United Kingdom and Canada to allow filings that meet their home-country requirements also to be acceptable in the other two countries. An experiment in certain Canadian offerings is in effect now. Given that the U.K. is a member of the European Community (EC), this may be considered by some as a first step on the way to accepting in North America security offerings that meet the diverse disclosure requirements of all the various EC countries.

We believe that, at a minimum, IASC accounting standards (IASC GAAP) should be adhered to by foreign companies registering securities in the United States. But we are unable to answer the resultant question of whether U.S. companies should be allowed also to follow IASC GAAP rather than FASB

GAAP when they register their securities in the United States. A yes answer would endorse some loss of information, a position no AIMR member wishes to support. A no answer implies special treatment for foreign companies to compete in U.S. capital markets without disclosing all that U.S. companies must, thus perpetuating noncomparable financial reports between U.S. and non-U.S. issuers. Furthermore, if the SEC were to accept IASC GAAP for all public companies, its reports would be noncomparable with those of private companies who (presumably) would continue to follow U.S. GAAP.

For the time being, in our opinion, the SEC should continue to require foreign companies to provide a reconciliation from the accounting standards followed in their home country to U.S. GAAP. We believe that foreign companies should be allowed and encouraged to adopt IASC GAAP, but that the reconciliation to U.S. GAAP should continue to be required at least until the IASC Improvements Project is completed. At that time, we shall need to reconsider our position.

**Frequency of Reporting.** In the United States, publicly owned companies are required to report quarterly on Form 10-Q filings with the SEC. Exchange regulations require listed firms to send quarterly reports directly to shareholders. Private companies also tend to report quarterly to their creditors and other financial statement users. In most other countries, financial reports are issued semi-annually; in a few countries, only annual reporting is the norm. Some people now advocate that the United States abolish its quarterly reporting requirement and regress to semi-annual or even annual reporting only.

AIMR unequivocally supports quarterly financial reporting and is opposed to any movement to eliminate it. Our arguments on that subject appear in more detail later in this report. At this point, we wish merely to point out that some of the impetus for the eradication of quarterly reporting results from the phenomenon of globalization. We believe that financial markets, both domestic and foreign, are best served by frequent and even-handed dissemination of information to the public. We urge the Congress of the United States, the SEC and its international counterpart—IOSCO—to heed the admonitions later in this report on the subject of quarterly reporting.

**Auditing or Other Forms of Enhancing Financial Statement Credibility.** In recent years, the IASC has received a great amount of attention as it attempts to codify a globally acceptable set of accounting standards. Alternatively, more people should become informed of the role of a parallel organization, the International Federation of Accountants and its Auditing Practices Committee, because its work is as necessary to the integrity of financial statements as is that of the IASC. As financial statements begin to conform to a worldwide GAAP, we need also to be able to rely on them.

Although we hold no brief for considering "made in America" audits supreme, we are aware that agreed-upon audit standards in this country—general standards, standards of fieldwork, and standards of reporting—are in some ways superior to those in some other parts of the world. In particular, we regard independence as an essential prerequisite to attestation. Yet there are countries where the law mandates that the auditor be a member of the corporate governing board. In some countries, the education requirements for auditors may be inadequate to keep them up to date with the electronic systems and the sophisticated financial affairs of multinational companies.

We believe that international agreement on auditing standards and practices would improve the standards of practice in all countries, including the United States and Canada. For example, the infamous collapse of the Bank for Credit and Commerce International indicates how a truly determined international renegade enterprise can shelter itself from effective auditing by hiding its records and conducting its corporate affairs in jurisdictions with less-than-strict financial regulation. We seek, together with professional accountants worldwide, to prevent a recurrence of that calamity.

**Preclude the "Lowest Common Denominator" Syndrome.** As globalization of accounting, disclosure, reporting frequency, and auditing standards proceeds, we must guard against the penchant to avoid difficult choices. Standards differ around the world in substance and in quality. It is always easier to lower the barriers than to raise them, thereby adopting the basest rule rather than the most elevated. AIMR stands behind those who are willing to make hard choices and raise the level in the majority of the world (including, in several instances, the United States and Canada) rather than acquiescing to the lowest common denominator. Likewise, we anticipate that standards setters, regulators, and professional accountants will aspire to raising global financial reporting to the highest and most useful level attainable.

## Quantum Increases in Computing Power and Access to It

One wonders if and when the pace of progress in computing will ever slow. Processing speeds and storage capacity continue to become available in large quantities and at low prices unheard of previously. A corollary is that computing also has been made available to individuals and has become portable. Where it all will lead ultimately is not for us to guess. Our task is to assess how it has and will change financial analysis and investment techniques as well as identify the implications of those effects for financial reporting.

The preceding section of this report deals with globalization of the securities industry. In many respects, that has been made possible by computing power aided by similar advances in telecommunications. As a result, money can be moved around the world quickly to take advantage of investment opportunities wherever and whenever they appear. Records can be updated instantly. Information may be formatted for computer processing and transmitted via modem or equivalent.

### Use of Data Bases and Quantitative Techniques.

Much financial data are to be found in data bases, some of which are publicly available while others are proprietary. Of the data bases publicly accessible in North America, one extreme is represented by Compustat, which contains financial statistics on more than 10,000 U.S. companies, organized by industry code and arranged in a standard financial statement format. At the other extreme is National Automated Accounting Retrieval System. It contains the actual text of the financial reports of more than 5,000 companies. Both of these data bases include several years of data. In between are an unlimited variety of specialized data bases offered by all sorts of vendors, including, among others, the FASB itself.

Use of data bases varies from analyst to analyst. Some analysts ignore them and continue to obtain their company and industry information from more traditional sources. Others use them in screening a large universe of companies to weed out those that do not meet certain criteria. The screening process often involves the use of financial ratios, and the program employed is generally concerned more with processing large quantities of data rather than performing sophisticated computations. Another group of analysts will use highly complex quantitative techniques to make portfolio selections and as a guide to other market transactions.

The implications for both financial analysis and financial reporting are profound. A common computer expression is, "garbage in, garbage out." Much of the analysis work performed by computers involves comparisons of company-specific data or of ratios constructed from those data. One needs to read but a few annual reports to realize that such comparisons are fraught with danger if made on the basis of unadjusted data. There are too many dissimilarities in how different companies record similar transactions, events, and happenings to draw any but rough comparisons from unadjusted data.

Some services, such as Compustat, attempt to adjust the data themselves; others do not. The need to adjust will be diminished and the quality of comparisons elevated to the extent that financial accounting standards produce financial statements that are consistent from period to period and comparable from company to company. That is a goal to be coveted, but analysts themselves should realize it will never be totally attained.

**The SEC's Electronic Data Gathering And Retrieval System.** We look forward to the imminent availability of the SEC's new method of making company filings available. Although it has been many years in development and subject to multiple delays, it promises to be a vast improvement over the present system. It will place documents in electronic storage and overcome the frequent problems of missing and misfiled documents now encountered by analysts or the agencies serving them. It will also dispense information faster than currently by placing a document in the data base when it is received. The SEC's initial plans are that it not be directly accessible by analysts; instead its contents will be marketed by vendors selected by the SEC. It promises to surpass all other data bases for its sheer quantity of information about public companies. Eventually, it may make even the most recalcitrant analyst into a data base user.

## Business Activities That Do Not Fit a Manufacturing/Mercantile Accounting Model

The traditional accounting model was developed originally to fit mercantile firms by matching to sales revenue the costs of products sold together with the other periodic costs of running the business. It also was grounded in the concept of the business entity. It was modified, through the aegis of cost accounting, to include manufacturing activities. That modification was less than perfect and often resulted in the need for additional information to be generated outside the accounting system for use in decision making and control. But for external reporting purposes, the fit was considered adequate and is being followed more or less faithfully today even though much business activity takes place for which the traditional accounting model is inadequate. We do not think that it should be discarded or replaced, but we believe that it is in need of some major modifications, as we specify in more detail later.

**Changes in Business Ownership.** Merger and acquisition activity ebbs and flows with economic cycles, but each pinnacle seems higher than the last.

Many people believe that existing values can be realized only when a transaction takes place, a major premise of accounting as practiced today. But this leads to certain financial statement anomalies. For example, when Firm A is purchased by Firm B, it is the assets and liabilities of Firm A that are recorded at their fair value, not those of Firm B. That is because those values are considered to have been validated by a transaction, even though the transaction was at a single price for the entire firm and cannot be a reliable measure of the specific value of any of its components. One could then argue that whatever techniques are used to place values on the individual assets and liabilities of Firm A could be used to restate the assets and liabilities of Firm B. If not, then we perhaps ought not to apply them to Firm A.

An even more difficult situation arises when Firm B acquires less than total ownership of Firm A. Under current practice, only the proportionate share of Firm A's assets and liabilities owned by Firm B are revalued, but all of Firm A's assets and liabilities— partially revalued, partially not—are consolidated with those of Firm B, none of whose assets and liabilities have been revalued. What a mélange! The result is a combination of historic and current values that only a mystic could sort out with precision.

The rise of highly leveraged transactions and the concomitant issuance of high-risk securities raises additional problems. Questions arise over the extent to which values that obviously exist (because lenders and others have invested in them) should be recognized in the financial statements. In many cases, we see accounting that differs because of the form of the underlying transaction, not its substance. Concurrently, we see differences in substance that are not reflected in the accounting.

In addition to the problem of when to recognize new values at the time of business combinations, we have the old one of when to derecognize values that no longer exist. It is difficult today to find a major company that has not during the three most recent years had at least one major writedown of asset values under the rubric of "restructuring charge" or some similar appellation. More times than not, these come as fourth quarter "surprises" to financial analysts. Not only do we need standards that make asset impairment writedowns more predictable, we also find it peculiar that many accountants deem writedowns to be good because they are "conservative" whereas writeups are not. It seems to us that whatever criteria are applied to determine writedowns would be every bit as verifiable and useful if also applied to writeups.

The matters discussed in this section currently have been and are addressed in several FASB Discussion Memoranda. We commend the Board for confronting them. Completion of the FASB's work on this subject is needed to eliminate the remarkable conceptual inconsistency in accounting in these areas and its exacerbation by intense business acquisition and combination activity.

### Rise in the Proportion of Economic Activity Conducted by the Service Sector.

Whether we like it or not, manufacturing and mercantile operations have become over time a smaller and smaller segment of the economies of the United States, Canada, and many other developed nations. Much of the value added by business enterprises in those economies now comes from services: business services, personal services, and financial services. These are businesses in which physical assets, plants, inventories, and the like, have little importance. In turn, traditional accounting-based performance measures have also suffered severely reduced usefulness. For example, return on invested capital is not a very meaningful measure in a law firm or accounting firm, or even an investment advisory firm, because so much of the capital is formed from human resources, inherently unmeasurable under current accounting precepts.

Service firms can be divided into two different categories: financial services and all others. The latter encompasses a variety of activities. Included therein are professional services (legal, accounting, architectural, etc.), business services (telecommunications and cable television, waste removal, etc.), entertainment in all its myriad forms including sports, and educational services provided by a variety of vendors. All of these endeavors have common implications for financial reporting. First, the value of the service often may have little relation to the cost of providing it. A different perspective would be that certain services are unique or otherwise protected from competition, as in the case of cable television. Conversely, some other services are marketed to a competitive extreme.

In all of these service companies, traditional measures of profitability, liquidity, productivity, solvency, and efficiency have lost some of their usefulness. The share of economic resources represented by plant and other tangible assets has diminished in size and importance, displaced by intangible assets arising from monopoly rights and other singularities, market shares and brand names, contractual and other stable relationships with clientele, and a host of others. In many cases, the future cash flows of the service firm depend on retaining personnel who are trained and competent to continue to provide services to existing customers and, even more important, to bring new customers to the business.

The problems in accounting for service-type firms are epitomized by the methods of accounting that apply to computer software firms. FASB

Statement 86 sets standards for accounting for the cost of computer software to be sold, leased, or otherwise marketed. Its reasoning is in accord with traditional accounting thought, but its result is to place on the balance sheet as an asset an amount that depicts neither the value of the software nor the total cost of developing it. Software revenue recognition is addressed in AICPA Statement of Position 91-1. It applies accounting for contracts more or less successfully to computer software development, but it gives unsatisfactory answers to the unique problem of a software vendor's continuing obligations to customers after installation. We do not fault either the FASB or the AICPA. They did the best they could in applying the current accounting model to a situation it was not designed to fit. Nor do we believe that the current accounting model should be discarded for one that is radically different. We are at this time merely pointing out the strains on it from applying it to new and different business activities. Our suggestions for change appear later in this report.

**Financial Services and the Proliferation of Financial Instruments.** Financial services firms, primarily financial institutions and other intermediaries, are like other service firms in that tangible assets are insignificant to them. But their other assets are different, being composed almost entirely of financial instruments. Most of those instruments represent diverse contractual arrangements with heterogeneous counterparties, with equity investments constituting the remainder. Financial firms also have substantial liabilities in the form of financial instruments. The success or failure of such a firm is to a large extent dependent on how well its management matches, from one side of the balance sheet to the other, maturities, yields, and other characteristics of its financial asset and liability positions. None of this is new.

What is new are two related matters of current and continuing concern. First is the proliferation of new and exotic financial instruments, many of which do not now appear on balance sheets or, if they do, understate the potential for loss that they engender. Analysts also are confounded by the interrelationships and complexity of financial instruments. For example, how can risks be assessed intelligently for a financial institution that is extensively arbitraged through contractual arrangements with multiple other financial institutions worldwide? Those risks are at least to be disclosed under the provisions of FASB Statement 105, but the disclosures are scattered throughout the financial statement notes and are completely understood only by relatively sophisticated and tenacious financial statement readers.

Complex and sophisticated financial instruments are used for a variety of purposes, and their propagation continues unabated. Some divide single instruments into component parts to serve the specialized needs of certain providers of capital who otherwise could not invest in a particular activity. Others bundle multiple instruments into a single package, again to serve specific investor demands. Many have been designed to shift risks to those willing to undertake them and provide hedging to their counterparties. Others have been designed and are used for more nefarious reasons, such as skirting the boundaries of accounting standards, rules, and practices. As additional standards are written, new instruments seem to be created to evade them. At least that is the perception of many financial analysts.

We commend the FASB for undertaking its gargantuan financial instruments project. In many of its facets, we are being forced to face up to the deficiencies arising from application of historic cost accounting to financial instruments. In the worst cases, historic cost accounting has allowed financial enterprises to manipulate reported income by recognizing gains (and, less frequently, losses) at will rather than when they occurred. Cognate to that is the resultant inclusion on balance sheets of historic costs that bear no relationship to their current value and that too many times conceal the fact that the financial instruments they purport to portray are "under water."

The second major issue pertaining to financial services is whether mark-to-market accounting is the remedy for the deficiencies of historic cost as applied to financial instruments. Some AIMR members support it wholeheartedly and believe that it should supplant historic cost on the financial statements. Others have reservations about or are opposed to market value accounting. None is opposed to disclosure of market values, and most believe that it is vital. Some urge caution to avoid disclosures that are incomplete or that imply that market value disclosure can easily be substituted for the historic valuations that appear on financial statements now. In sum, we are agreed that information about market values is important, but we differ on the degree of importance and the extent to which they should be incorporated in financial reports. This topic is discussed at greater length later in this report.

**Growth in the Size of Institutional Ownership of Securities.** Since World War II, the proportion of securities, particularly common stock, owned by institutions has grown continuously. At the end of September, 1991, only 54.5 percent of total equities were held by households, down from 91.3 percent in 1950.[1] The rest are held by mutual funds, pension plans, philanthropic and educational organizations, etc. The rise of institutional ownership is subject matter for a different report than this, but it does have implications for financial

---

[1]*Fact Book for the Year 1991.* (New York: New York Stock Exchange, Inc., 1992), p. 28.

analysis.

A notable consequence of the rise of institutional investors is the increased need for financial reports written for and directed to the professionals who actually select or otherwise recommend the securities owned by institutions. They should be viewed as the primary audience for financial statements. The needs of individual investors are often cited in discussions of financial reporting. But the acumen, cognizance, and savvy of individual investors is often underestimated. It would be scandalous to deprive professional investment advisors, portfolio managers, and other financial analysts of information they need on the flimsy grounds that those data might confuse individuals who do not understand accounting. After all, those who profess to use financial reports bear some responsibility to educate themselves on how to read them.

# QUALITATIVE CHARACTERISTICS
# OF FINANCIAL STATEMENTS

There is general agreement that accounting and other financial data should have certain characteristics. The Financial Accounting Standards Board's Statement of Financial Accounting Concepts No. 2, "Qualitative Characteristics of Accounting Information" (FAC 2) creates two groups of these characteristics under the headings "relevance" and "reliability." That grouping is appropriate because in many cases the format and content of accounting data require a trade-off between the two. Certainly financial analysts desire information that is both relevant and reliable, but their bias is towards relevance. In a phrase, analysts prefer information that is equivocally right rather than precisely wrong. Inexact measures of contemporaneous economic values generally are more useful than fastidious historic records of past exchanges. A short discussion of several characteristics of accounting quality and our views of them follows.

## Relevance

In an ideal world, the most relevant accounting data would be those that reported assets and liabilities in a way that would allow analysts to impute the future cash flows emanating from them individually and collectively. The certainty embodied in that world does not exist. In fact, if it did, there would be no need for analysis. Therefore, we must strive for an accounting model that reflects the degree of uncertainty that besets a particular enterprise, the consequence of which is a valuation system that is eclectic. Some assets, such as receivables, are stated explicitly at the amounts expected to be received in cash. Other assets, such as certain types of securities, are stated at market value, implicitly the amount of cash that could be received. Some assets are stated at the amounts paid for them (historic cost) pending receipt of evidence that they are worth some other amount (realization). Some assets may not appear in the financial statements at all because there is no sensible way to report them.

Historic costs are sunk costs and there is little disagreement that they are often irrelevant to financial decisions. But there is considerable debate as to whether they should be totally replaced by more relevant current values, whether current values should be provided only as supplementary data, what version of current value should be used, and how (in the absence of a firm-specific exchange or organized auction market) current value should be determined. There also is some opinion among AIMR members that determination of the current values of specific assets is a function of financial analysis, not financial reporting. However, almost all would agree that so-called "lower of cost or market" methods are neither informative nor useful. They are based on the untenable premise that market value is a good accounting measure when it is lower than historic cost, but not when it is higher. The best argument that can be made in favor of lower of cost or market is that it does reveal market values when they are lower than cost, thus divulging important information on certain asset impairments.

## Reliability: General

The two primary components of reliability are verifiability and representational faithfulness. The former refers to the likelihood that different accountants, availing themselves of the same evidence, will draw similar conclusions. The latter refers to the likelihood that the accounting measure depicts accurately the nature of the object being measured.

## Reliability: Verifiability

This characteristic is intimately related to the attest function. For financial reports to be useful, they must be trustworthy. The report of the independent auditor is essential. The auditor, however, can verify only that which can be documented or confirmed. Perhaps that is one reason for the extensive amount of detailed guidance provided with current accounting standards. As the standards-setting process has infiltrated areas in which the measurements are less than precise (pensions and other postemployment benefits, financial instruments, recognition of fee revenues, etc.), the rules have become more detailed. Detailed rules may also be perceived as necessary to serve the needs of both financial statement preparers and their independent auditors. Verifiability implies that two unrelated parties considering the same facts independently will draw similar conclusions. It is possible that detailed rules are now the only way to inculcate verifiability into measurements that otherwise are subject to honest differences of opinion. Can better ways be found? We hope so and are heartened by the issuance of FASB Statement 109, "Accounting for Income Taxes," which we regard as a step in the right direction.

Another aspect of verifiability is knowledge of its absence. Most accounting numbers have an appearance of precision. But other than contemporaneous exchanges involving cash, accounting numbers are determined by estimates of various degrees of inexactitude. Analysts need to know how indefinite those numbers are, and they need to know the degree to which the same economic event or condition could have been reported differently using alternative measurement methods. More information of that sort incorporated in financial reports would be exceedingly welcome.

### Reliability: Representational Faithfulness

Assets and liabilities are probable future economic benefits and claims against those benefits, and users of financial statements expect to see them depicted accurately. There are two aspects to representing them faithfully. One is to select the appropriate attribute to measure; the other is to measure it accurately. There are too many examples to cite them all, but one may be instructive.

Under current accounting practice, intangible assets are recorded at cost only when they are purchased from another entity, either separately or as part of a business combination. The effect is that self-developed intangibles are not recorded at all or at the nominal amounts spent to assure monopoly rights. Furthermore, the costs of both purchased and self-developed intangibles are amortized over arbitrary future time spans, even though their value may decrease in some other pattern or, in many cases, increase as the enterprise makes additional expenditures to maintain or enhance their value. Those accounting practices cause severe noncomparability between and among companies.

Also, regardless of whether intangibles are recorded at the cost of purchasing them or at the nominal amounts to develop them internally, many of the future benefits to be obtained from them are more speculative and conjectural than those to be received from tangible assets which ordinarily have some value in alternative use. So only at the date on which purchased intangibles are acquired do the financial statements assuredly reflect amounts that purport to be representationally faithful of economic reality. Moreover, there may well be no accounting measure capable of expressing well over time that the sole economic benefit of intangible assets is their potential contribution to the future cash flows of the enterprise. Our specific recommendations for accounting for intangible assets are discussed later in this report.

## Timeliness

Although FAC 2 categorizes timeliness as a subset of relevance, it has an importance to analysts that merits attention of its own. As we argue above, financial information is useful only when it is disseminated quickly, fairly, and widely because the digestion of such information by analysts is what makes markets efficient. In the United States and Canada, this has been embodied in the practice of companies issuing financial statements quarterly supplemented by press releases and, in the U.S., Form 8-K disclosures for important events occurring between reports.

Recently there has been vocal criticism of the practice of quarterly financial reporting. It has been accused of causing managers of U.S. businesses to focus on short-term results and of neglecting those activities whose worth would be greater over a longer time. Investors have been blamed for calling portfolio managers to account for their quarterly performances and portfolio managers for responding to them.

Ironically, the financial markets are increasingly influenced by the investment activities of pension trusts, whose corporate sponsors are managed by the same persons who protest that frequent interim reports force them to manage for the short term. Also, it is unlikely that rational investors will punish a firm for undertaking projects that promise extraordinary long-term payoffs as long as that firm is willing and able to communicate to those investors its strategy and tactics.

A further irony is that business managers themselves often are compensated or otherwise rewarded for short-term performance, measured either by accounting numbers or by the market performance of their employer's securities. Relief from so-called "short termism" is more likely to be successfully effected through changes in corporate governance, including fundamental and radical changes in the paradigm used to reward certain executives, than by abolishing one of the most important sources of analytic information available.

A collateral benefit of frequent financial reporting is that it diminishes opportunities for trading on privileged information, a practice AIMR and other responsible members of the investment community deplore. The longer a company waits to release information to the public, the more likely it is that the information will become known sooner to a small and select group that can use it to trade for its own benefit. Even under current disclosure rules, which many find draconian, financial information has from time to time been intercepted or diverted on its way to dissemination.

## Neutrality

In addition to timely dissemination, fairness also requires neutrality—presentation of data that are without bias. Investors buy and sell securities. Financial reports should inform traders on both sides of a transaction in such a way that neither is favored. Much of what applies here was discussed above under the heading of relevance. Historic costs, even more so lower of cost or market procedures, tend to introduce bias in favor of buyers of securities by suppressing good news while revealing the bad straight away. The absence of adjustments to reflect price changes, even as supplementary information only, in North American accounting standards institutes a bias that varies in proportion to (1) the rate of price change, (2) the dispersion of those changes among the various goods and services traded, and (3) the holding period for assets whose prices change.

# BROAD TOPICS OF CURRENT IMPORTANCE
# TO ANALYSTS

In this section, we address several financial reporting matters that are of current and continuing importance to investment managers and analysts. Some of the subjects considered herein embody difficult questions for both financial reporting and financial analysis. On some of those questions AIMR members hold strong and unified views. On others, their opinions are divided, although their individual views may be no less strongly held.

## Mark-to-Market Accounting: Value versus Valuation

Former SEC Chairman Richard Breeden once said that financial reports should begin with the phrase "Once upon a time . . ." His remark certainly was made with pejorative intent, given his many public statements in favor of recording financial assets at their market value, so-called "mark to market" accounting. In addition to the public advocacy of mark-to-market accounting by ex-Chairman Breeden, there have been other moves in that direction both in the United States and Canada, as well as abroad. The Financial Accounting Standards Board (FASB), in its financial instruments project, has issued Statement of Financial Accounting Standard No. 107 (FAS 107), which requires disclosure of the market value of many financial instruments. The FASB also has suggested market values as potentially appropriate measures in its discussion memorandum "Recognition and Measurement of Financial Instruments." Members of the Accounting Standards Board in the United Kingdom also have expressed strong support for using market values in financial reports.

AIMR members have different views on market values. Virtually all favor disclosure of market values, at least for financial instruments. No one seems to believe that disclosure alone could be detrimental to analysts' interests, and all but a few believe that disclosure would be beneficial. Most are opposed to *replacing* historic cost with market values, but a significant minority favors such a move. Most oppose extending mark-to-market accounting from financial assets to real assets, although a small number does not. Almost all agree that if mark-to-market accounting were to be mandated, it should be applied with equanimity to both the left-hand side and the right-hand side of the balance sheet. All agree that it is only specific identifiable assets and liabilities that should be marked to market; determination of the market values of entire firms is the business of financial analysis, not financial reporting. Mark-to-market accounting has many ramifications that have different amounts of persuasive power on individual analysts.

**Knowing What Market Value Is.**  It is axiomatic that it is better to know what something is worth now than what it was worth at some moment in the past. However, that is easier said than done. Much has been made of the fact that securities firms and mutual funds mark their balance sheets to market daily. The question is asked why banks and other financial institutions cannot do the same. The answer is that it can be done but with conceptual and practical difficulties that do not exist for security firms and mutual funds.

Balance sheets that are marked to market now are done so on a daily basis. They are never out of date, because they are replaced by a new balance sheet every single business day. Other enterprises issue financial statements less frequently, quarterly and annually. Furthermore, it takes some time after the balance sheet date to prepare and disseminate it. By the time the balance sheet reaches the analyst, it already is out of date. Historic cost itself is in reality historic market value, the amount of a past transaction engaged in by the firm. Some argue that if we are to be presented with market values that are bound to be historic by the time they arrive, we are better off with older but transaction-based historic cost.

The counter-arguments to that line of reasoning are two. First, many historic costs are seriously out of date. They may have little relation to the current market value of assets, whereas the balance sheet market values (which are only slightly out-of-date) still will have a good amount of relevance. Second, market value data are comparable. If all enterprises mark their balance sheets to market on the same date, they are all out-of-date by the same interval. Historic cost data are never comparable on a firm-to-firm basis because the costs were incurred at different dates by different firms (or even within a single firm).

There is no financial analyst who would not want to know the market value of individual assets and liabilities. There are many, however, who believe that those values are essentially unknowable.

**Applicability Limited by Measurement Problems.**  When the term "market value" is used, one is inclined to conjure up a mental picture of the busy trading floors of the New York Stock Exchange or the Chicago Board of Trade, frenzied with the activity of bringing together the effects of supply and demand on innumerable well-informed traders. A variety of equity securities, debt instruments, and commodities have their values continually being revised by frequent trades in well-functioning auction markets. Many other assets, including a myriad of financial instruments, do not trade frequently, and when they do trade the amounts and prices of those exchanged can deviate considerably over short periods of time. Supply and demand for a large number of financial assets is so thin as to defy determining their market values at any moment with a great deal of precision.

An alternate approach is to determine the market rate of interest at which to discount a given stream of cash flows expected to emanate from a particular financial instrument or portfolio of similar instruments. This might work with financial instruments that are securities, such as bonds, where the rates at which more popular issues trade could be applied to less frequently traded issues of the same credit quality. But even there one could infer that the rate on the marketable issue probably would be lower than that of a bond that is harder to liquidate. We also encounter the problem of determining the market rate of interest for financial instruments that do not trade, such as portfolios of consumer or business loans. How can we ensure comparability among a vast number of country banks choosing to measure with the same interest rate when they may have different costs of funds and local or regional variations in business conditions and credit risk?

Although our experience in the securities industry indicates to us that mark-to-market measures lack a good amount of reliability, one exception is marketable equity securities. As they are defined by Financial Accounting Standard No. 12, "Accounting for Certain Marketable Securities"—now superseded by Financial Accounting Standard No. 115 (FAS 115)—they have market values that are relatively easily determined by frequent trades in markets of sizable breadth and depth. All but one member of AIMR's Financial Accounting Policy Committee (FAPC) agreed that those securities should be reported at market value. The FAPC's view is based also on the unique characteristic of equity securities that they provide no contractually specified future cash payments.[1] Therefore, in their case, expected or hoped-for changes in market value are much if not all of the reason for investing in them. Recently issued FAS 115 goes part of the way by requiring marketable equity securities to be reported at market value, but using historic cost as the basis for recognition of gain or loss for most such securities. We

---

[1]This recommendation also applies to preferred stocks, even though they have a specified dividend amount or rate. That dividend is a ceiling, not a floor, on the amount to be paid; the preferred dividend itself constitutes a preference not a claim. The FAPC is on record, in previous comments to the FASB, as advocating that a preferred stock carrying a mandatory payment requirement be recorded and reported as a liability.

support the valuation but not the gain/loss recognition provisions of FAS 115.

Debt securities present a different situation. Many investors in these securities have little interest in the day-to-day changes in quoted prices. They hold such securities primarily in anticipation of collecting their future cash proceeds. The vast majority of debt security holders are financial institutions that seek to match streams of cash inflows from investments to their obligations payable in cash outflows. A basic principle of managing a financial intermediary is to minimize interest rate risk by linking financial asset investments to financial instrument liabilities. The process is best characterized as being one step short of hedging. Until methods are available to determine with reliability the market values of *all* the related financial liabilities, we cannot support a unilateral marking to market of the assets alone.

We are very aware of the fact that some institutions, in particular certain failed savings associations, have engaged in gains trading ("cherry picking," to some) in their bond investment portfolios. That leaves a portfolio primarily constituted of bonds whose market price is less than cost; the portfolio is said to be "under water." This objectionable practice would be eliminated by mark-to-market accounting under which gains and losses would be recognized as they occur, rather than as the effect of an exchange. Furthermore, whether investments in bonds are accounted for at cost, at market, or otherwise, the reported amounts of gains and losses should be separated from other revenues and expenses on the income statement so that financial analysts and others can both detect and evaluate them. If that procedure were to be followed, then under current GAAP,[2] gains trading should be evident to an astute analyst who looks closely both at the institution's sources of earnings and its disclosures of the market values of portfolios being carried at cost.

**How to Implement Mark-to-Market Accounting.** What would be the scope of mark-to-market accounting if it should be employed? Will it apply to all assets or only some? both assets and liabilities? all assets and some liabilities? Will it apply to all industries or only to some? Will it apply differently to different types of companies? These are the several broad questions that at least have to be considered before we plunge into the unknown.

---

[2]FAS 115 makes the requisite data for analysis more readily available than before, but we do not believe it represents an improvement in either recognition or measurement. We also believe that it is unjust to mandate a costly change in accounting for well-managed institutions to atone for the misconduct of others.

We start by considering a recent and current problem: how to value the bond portfolios of financial intermediaries. At the urging of the SEC, the problem was deliberated at length by the Accounting Standards Executive Committee (AcSEC) of the American Institute of Certified Public Accountants (AICPA), which issued several exposure drafts of position papers. When those efforts proved unsuccessful, the problem was passed on to the FASB, which issued FAS 115. Many observers note that marking to market only the bond investment portfolio introduces to reported earnings[3] a volatility that does not really exist because it is in effect canceled by *unrecognized* changes in liabilities having similar interest rate risk. However, counterpart liabilities cannot be identified that *specifically* relate to a bond portfolio. Thus, one is led to conclude that mark-to-market could only work if it were applied to all assets and liabilities. In financial institutions, that entails all the measurement difficulties discussed above.

It also forces consideration of the valuation of core deposits. Theoretically, there is no way in which a liability that must be paid at face amount on demand should have a market different from its nominal amount. But sometimes it does. This has been borne out by prices paid to acquire financial intermediaries. Even more dramatic evidence has come via recent "sales" of core deposits alone. The "sale" involves the acquiring institution accepting core deposit liabilities of a certain stated amount in exchange for receiving assets of a lesser amount. The valuation of core deposits is controversial, and it appears unlikely that recognition of their market value will be allowed, either directly or through recognition of a core deposit intangible asset. Even if recognition were permitted, how would the value of core deposits that are not traded be measured?

For non-financial enterprises, how should mark-to-market accounting be applied, or should it? If financial services enterprises are required to mark their financial instruments to market, should not all firms that hold or issue financial instruments also be required to record them at market value? For some such enterprises that hold large and stable interests in other enterprises, doing so would introduce a volatility into reported earnings that seems unrelated to the economic accomplishment of the period. But most assets of such firms are non-financial, either tangible (such as inventory and plant) or intangibles of various sorts. Marking these to market would require solutions to different measurement problems, the pursuit of which unfortunately ceased

---

[3]In FAS 115, the FASB has evaded the issue by prescribing that a portion of the debt portfolio be marked to market, but without recognition of its effect on earnings, a position with which no FAPC members agrees.

when the FASB issued Financial Accounting Standard No. 89.[4] The concept of measuring the current cost (or some other current market value) of tangible assets is relatively straightforward, but its application engenders practical difficulties and often produces less-than-precise measurements. Answers with respect to intangible assets are not so obvious, and we devote a separate section of this report below to their consideration.

**Effect of Market Value Changes on Trend Analysis.** Many financial analysts oppose mark-to-market accounting because of its potential effects on their analysis of trends. Much current analysis of financial intermediaries focuses on changes in balance sheet items stated at historic cost. Trend analysis, in particular, requires comparable numbers period by period. Historic costs allow analysts to assess changes in a financial intermediary's financial position without having first to remove the confounding effects on that position of exogenous economic events. For example, analytic disaggregation of a loan portfolio by geographic area, purpose of loan (commercial real estate, consumer credit), and so on is essential to understanding the risks and exposures of a financial institution. Many analysts seek data that reveal the changes in the intermediary's portfolio resulting from transactions, excluding the effect of changes imposed by the market. In addition, they wish to compare historic yields on investments in securities and other financial instruments with the institution's overall and regional cost of funds. Those analysts feel that important data would be irretrievably lost if historic costs were supplanted in the financial statements themselves by mark-to-market accounting.

**Effect of Market Value Changes on Income.** No matter how well mark-to-market accounting could be implemented and applied judiciously to matched assets and liabilities, it still would increase significantly the volatility of reported earnings. Some argue that the volatility exists and that a primary benefit of mark-to-market accounting is that real volatility would be revealed. We agree. But the question of how business enterprises and the capital markets are to deal with it remains.

As financial reporting is practiced today, financial managers have much discretion over the recognition of changes in value by astute timing of exchange transactions and by the adoption of artful allocation procedures.

---

[4]This standard removed the requirement, under FAS 33, for disclosure of supplementary information on changing prices. Although FAS 89 encourages such disclosures, they have rarely been seen in U.S. financial reporting since the requirement was removed.

Mark-to-market accounting would take away much of that discretion. Even where the relative influence of market value changes is small overall, at the margin it has the propensity to make earnings exceedingly unpredictable, a disconcerting fact for enterprises trying to minimize their capital costs by reporting smooth and growing earnings.

Some analysts are quite willing to accept the increases in reported income volatility that would be produced under mark-to-market accounting. Many even would welcome it. They argue that the effects on a particular enterprise of general economic conditions and financial market movements are relevant and vital to their assessments of the enterprise's economic status and progress over time. They may not yet be ready to do away with historic cost entirely, but they look forward to the opportunity of integrating FAS 107 data into their evaluations and forecasts now that they have become generally available.

One method for dealing with changing market values and their effect on income would be for the FASB to generate accounting standards that put into practice the concept of comprehensive income that appears in Concepts Statement No. 6. As defined in Paragraphs 73-77 of that statement, comprehensive income would encompass all changes in owners' equity exclusive of transactions with owners themselves. It would also be disaggregated into a variety of basic components and intermediate components. Thus the effect of exogenous events such as market value changes would be separated from the effect of endogenous productive activities. If market value changes were reported separately and clearly, their effect isolated, then their unpredictability would assume a lesser importance as it was assessed separately from productive activities.

**Prognosis for Mark-to-Market Accounting.** A few financial analysts and investment managers are unequivocally opposed to (and a few are unalterably in favor of) mark-to-market accounting. But most have adopted a wait-and-see attitude. It is difficult to forsake historic cost when it is uncertain that its replacement will accomplish what its advocates promise. FAS 107, which became effective for fiscal periods ending after December 15, 1992, requires disclosure of the market value of many financial instrument assets but only some of the related liabilities. We anticipate that many of the problems set forth in the preceding discussion will be encountered in its application. We welcome the opportunity to deal with them in a realistic setting without having to make a total commitment and changeover to mark-to-market accounting. We also expect that at least some of the experience gained from applying FAS 107 to financial instruments may be transferable later to nonfinancial assets and liabilities.

We regret that we are unable herein to report a consensus among FAPC members on the mark-to-market issue. We *are* able to report the scope and nature of the different viewpoints held by knowledgeable and sincere financial analysts. We need more information, however, and we are acting to obtain it. As a result of comment on the exposure draft of this report, AIMR has authorized a comprehensive study and report of the opinions of the entire AIMR membership on the role of market values in financial reporting. That study is now in its early stages and is being conducted by a subcommittee of the FAPC.

Finally, we note that mark-to-market accounting is intended to apply to individual assets and/or liabilities, either singly or in portfolios of homogeneous components. Despite our overall opposition to its imminent adoption, we consider it to be appropriately within the domain of the accounting function. On the other hand, when it comes to the valuation of business enterprises— either singly, in groups, or by components—we rightfully regard that as the province of financial analysis and a matter beyond the scope of financial reporting.

## Accounting for Intangible Assets

An earlier part of this report discusses implications for financial reporting of the rise in the proportion of economic activity attributable to the service sector. One ramification is its exacerbation of the persistent and vexing question of how to account for intangible assets. Service businesses are, with certain notable exceptions (such as telecommunications), generally labor intensive. These firms have few tangible assets and in many cases have balance sheets that under conventional accounting show meager or even negative owners' equity. In fact, however, they may possess sizable unrecorded economic resources in the form of anticipated future cash flows. Yet under traditional accounting methods, the value of those future cash flows is recorded only when (1) the cash flows are acquired in a purchase transaction with an unrelated party or (2) the anticipated cash finally is received. On the other hand, equity investors and lenders are forced to acknowledge the value of future cash flows to make sensible investment and lending decisions in competition with other rational suppliers of capital. Our views on this matter are set forth below.

**Nature of the Problem.** All economic value must ultimately result in cash inflows. In fact, it is future cash flows to which both equity investors and lenders look for a return on and return of their investments. Tangible assets offer an additional measure of comfort in that they usually but not always have some value at liquidation even though it may be modest. Furthermore, tangible assets are, without significant exception, acquired in exchange transactions with outsiders and, except for business combinations, are usually acquired individually or in groups of related items. Even when acquired in a basket purchase, it usually is not difficult to obtain competent data to allow their values to be reported separately. As a result, there ordinarily is little problem in recording at least the initial values of tangible assets. The same is true of intangible assets (patents, franchises, etc.) purchased separately.

Major problems arise with accounting for intangible assets that either are self-developed or acquired in a business combination. Other problems emanate from intangibles whose sole value comes from their ability to enhance the cash flows of a going concern. For example, how are analysts sensibly to compare two firms, one of which has developed strong brand names through sizable expenditures that have not been capitalized (say, the Proctor and Gamble Company), the other of which has grown by purchasing the brand names of others (say, RJR Nabisco)? How are analysts to find useful the financial statements of cable television and other media firms that have significantly negative net worths because they have borrowed against future cash flows and used the proceeds either to cover reported losses or to make payments to stockholders?[5]

**Sources of Future Cash Flows.** Intangible assets comprise all sorts of contractual, institutional, and informal arrangements, all of which are characterized by associated expectations of future cash inflows. Many of these values are attributable to human beings who are talented, well-trained, acculturated, or otherwise able and willing to contribute to the enterprise's economic well-being. Arrangements between the firm and its employees vary. Some, mainly senior managers and others who make unique contributions, serve under individual contracts. Some of those contracts may contain provisions that activate sizable payments at or after the individual's separation from the firm, so-called "golden parachutes" and similar arrangements. At the other end of the scale are collective bargaining agreements with unions and other worker organizations. In between are the ordinary day-to-day, month-to-month continuances of employment and service.

---

[5]In 1988, King World Productions, syndicators of the television programs *Jeopardy*, *Wheel of Fortune*, and *Oprah Winfrey*, was reported to have a $30 million negative net worth for exactly that reason. *Forbes*, July 11, 1988, page 83.

Future cash flows may also be attributed to franchises. That term is used in its broadest sense to include not only contractual arrangements but also other exclusive accesses to customers. A brand name might be said to be a "franchise." For example, one thinks of the position of the Campbell name in canned soup, H.J. Heinz in ketchup, or Bayer in aspirin. Anther example of an exclusivity is a long-established reputation, such as those carried by the "Big Six" accounting firms, certain major law firms, advertising agencies, actuaries, consultants and a host of other professional services providers. Health care organizations are very likely to have franchises arising from both their reputations and their proximity to patients. A news distributorship in New York City's Manhattan is worth more than one in Manhattan, Kansas. The examples could go on and on.

In many cases, expectations of future cash flows may dissipate in the face of competition and are able to continue to flourish only if the enterprise continues to support them with attention and expenditures. Alternatively, exclusive rights may be obtained either under law (patents, copyrights, trademarks, etc.) or by contract. An enterprise may contract for a franchise (in the narrow sense of the word), for human services, for services to be provided by another organization, or for the rights to use real assets (plant and equipment) for limited periods of time.

All of the above are intended to be an illustrative but not exhaustive list of the incredible variety of sources of intangible value. All of them illustrate cases of valuable assets that, with two exceptions, are not recorded. One exception is when the asset is purchased in an arms-length exchange transaction. The other exception is for certain lease agreements that meet one of the conditions that qualify them as capital leases.

**A Note on Stock Compensation Cost.** Unlike many other portions of the financial reporting process, the issue of stock-based compensation has been one of low priority to financial analysts and money managers. That is because stock options, the type of stock compensation plan for which changes in accounting are contemplated, have no direct consequential effect on the enterprise's future cash flows from operations. Therefore, we have not been proactive in the debate on this issue. That said, however, we do have views on it that we wish to make known.

First, we strongly believe that stock options have value, that they are used to compensate managers, and that they should be recognized and measured as compensation expense in the financial statements, if practicable. We asserted earlier in this report that financial statements should be complete and that disclosure is not an acceptable substitute for recognition and measurement.

We have yet to be persuaded that measurement of stock compensation is sufficiently reliable as to be practicable. The methods proposed by the FASB rely on modifications of option valuation models that were developed for quite different purposes. Furthermore, their extensive use of estimates, including but not limited to future stock price volatility, disturbs many of us who as investment professionals find prediction of stock price volatility a daunting task. AIMR's FAPC has yet to establish its position on the measurement issue.

We are unable in this document to discuss fully the entire stock compensation issue. However, we can comment on the often-heard argument that the dilutive effect of stock options on earnings per share (EPS) makes redundant the measurement of compensation expense on the income statement. We disagree. EPS is not an accounting number; it is a financial ratio, a tool of financial analysis. The only reason its computation and disclosure is governed by an accounting standard is to produce EPS numbers that are comparable across enterprises and to preclude the egregious abuses that prevailed before the standard was issued. The calculation of EPS requires a numerator (earnings) and a denominator (shares). It is the business of accounting to measure and report earnings, the numerator. And, as we note above, the question of stock compensation is one of income determination. Only after that is settled need we turn our attention to the question of the number of shares (actual or potential) over which those earnings are to be spread.

**The Problem of Goodwill.** We are not concerned with the theory of goodwill except as it pertains to the usefulness of financial statements to analysts. We view goodwill as the amount that an enterprise as a whole is worth in excess of the values of its individual assets less individual liabilities. We are wholly in agreement with the Accounting Principles Board Opinion No. 16 with respect to the computation of goodwill.[6] We also agree that there is no reliable valuation of it in the absence of an exchange transaction involving controlling interest in an entire enterprise. We balk at the notion of goodwill being recorded without the authentication of a transaction.

What we disagree with is the Accounting Principles Board Opinion No. 17,

---

[6]Most published statements use the term "cost in excess of net assets acquired" where we use the term "goodwill." APBO 16 designates goodwill to be the excess of cost over the *fair value* (emphasis added) of all identifiable assets minus the *fair value* (emphasis added) of identifiable liabilities. In many other parts of the world, the term "goodwill" is used to designate the excess of cost over the *book value* of the net assets acquired. We believe the latter definition accurately describes accounting practice in certain jurisdictions but that it is not applicable to the present discussion.

which allows purchased goodwill to linger on the balance sheet for up to 40 years. Once it has been established for the record how much was paid to acquire goodwill, it ought to be removed from the list of assets forthwith.[7] That would remove a major impediment to comparing companies whose economic statuses are relatively similar but whose balance sheets are not. It is a drastic solution to the problem of noncomparability, but it is preferable to allowing other firms to record self-developed goodwill.

One might ask whether a goodwill write-off should appear on the income statement or go directly to owners' equity. Regardless of the answer, a more appropriate question is *where* on the income statement or *where* in the owner's equity section it should emerge. We believe that it should appear on the income statement as part of comprehensive income, and that this is another instance that illustrates the need for the FASB to develop standards for reporting comprehensive income. Cumulative amounts of goodwill write-offs also should be reported as a separate component of shareholders' equity together with complete disclosure of the changes in those amounts during each of the periods covered by the financial report.

**Contractual Arrangements.** Contractual arrangements are quite opposite from goodwill. We refer here to what are commonly called executory contracts, those awaiting performance by both parties. With the exception of capital leases, executory contracts are not recorded in financial statements and are disclosed only when they are material and not in the ordinary course of business. We have observed the machinations that often accompany the classification of lease agreements. We also are overwhelmed by the excessive volume of extremely detailed accounting definitions, procedures, and rules designed to foil such intrigues.

We suggest a standard that would be far simpler but broader in its application. We would require capitalization of all executory contracts with an initial term in excess of one year.[8] That would eliminate many of the problems attendant on lease accounting. More important, it would place on the balance sheet at least some of the quite real intangible assets that do not now appear. For example, in the case of King World Productions (see footnote

---

[7]Both the IASC and the Accounting Standards Board in the United Kingdom have proposed five-year amortization periods. That would be an enormous improvement over practice in the United States, but it still is an arbitrary procedure that lacks theoretical support. We prefer the current U.K. practice of immediate write-off.

[8]We understand that the accounting standard we advocate in this paragraph has been introduced in Australia, and it is reported to be a significant improvement over previous practice there.

9), it would allow recording as assets contractual rights with television stations with a corresponding liability to produce programming in the future.[9] We see that as not significantly different from capital lease accounting. We believe that employment contracts with executives and key employees also should be capitalized, even if performance cannot be compelled. If the employee resigns, the remaining equal amounts of intangible asset and obligation to pay wages would be removed from the balance sheet. If the employee is discharged, the remaining intangible asset would be a loss to the extent that the enterprise continued to be liable either for future compensation to the employee or for a settlement.

**Discovery Values.** Some years ago, the SEC initiated an experiment with "reserve recognition accounting" for oil- and gas-producing firms. It never got beyond the stage of supplemental data, and it entailed many practical and conceptual problems. Yet many analysts found that the information it generated, although primitive, was both unique and useful for valuation purposes. Portions of it remain in the disclosure requirements for oil- and gas-producing activities under Statement of Financial Accounting Standard No. 69. AIMR would like to see additional research on reserve recognition accounting as a prelude to a reconsideration of it as a possible replacement for current methods.

Both the "successful efforts" and "full cost" methods in use today are seriously impaired by their implicit assumption that part or all of the cost of exploration is a decent measure of the value of that which is discovered. Reserve recognition accounting, if feasible, would bring financial reports closer to the economic reality of how wealth is created not only in the oil and gas industry, but also in other types of enterprises in which significant values are created by "discovery." It has the strength of focusing on and reporting how discovery creates wealth and how other activities, such as production, refining, and delivery, enhance it.

**Costs to Create Intangible Assets.** We are not enamored of recording self-developed intangible assets unless their values are readily apparent. We consider the cost of creating them to be so often unrelated to their actual value as to be irrelevant in the investment evaluation process. Furthermore, it usually

---

[9]We do not anticipate that revenue recognition from productive activities would be affected by the recognition of the rights and obligations under executory contracts, other than the effect of recognizing the accretion of interest. In fact, it should not be. The standards for the *measurement* of revenue ought to be independent of the standards for the *recognition* of assets and liabilities.

is next to impossible to determine in any sensible or codifiable manner exactly which costs provide future benefit and which do not. For example, even though we would record the contractual amounts of employment agreements, we would not go so far as to capitalize the costs of training and developing human resources.

We cannot quarrel with capitalization of the costs of intangible assets that are *purchased*. In that case, the cost is the value of the asset: No heroic or outlandish assumption is required. However, to approach comparability with firms that have created similar intangibles with their own resources, we recommend amortization of the purchased variety over economic lives that we expect will be short. In most cases, a purchased intangible will maintain its value only if it is tended and cared for by the type of expenditures that create self-developed ones. A better way of looking at it is that if the purchased intangible is not maintained, it will be exhausted quickly, not to be replaced by a self-developed one.

We reiterate our strong feeling that goodwill should not be recognized except briefly and only when it is determined by the exchange price for an entire enterprise.

**The Importance of Cash Flows.** The discussion above makes it clear that intangible assets derive their value from the prospects they engender for future cash flows and that it is difficult or impossible in many cases to obtain a sufficiently reasonable measure of their value to place on the balance sheet. Therefore, it is important in extremis for financial reports to disclose clearly the amounts and sources of past cash flows. The ultimate test of the value of an intangible asset is whether it contributes to the stream of cash entering the firm. This is exactly the reasoning implicit in Financial Accounting Standard No. 2, "Accounting for Research and Development Costs." Because the expectation of future benefits from research expenditures is so uncertain, their value cannot be recorded in advance. We must wait until they are received in cash.

Not only do we have to know the source of cash flows from intangible assets in detail, we also have to know how likely it is that they will continue and at what rate. While the flows continue, we need to know what is being done with them. Are they being distributed or reinvested? Are the reinvestments in kind or are they a divergence from past practice? Much of the needed cash flow information requires both disaggregation of historic data and candid management discussion of the future. We speak later in this report at greater length about other aspects of the usefulness of the cash flow statement.

**Conclusions about Intangible Assets.** Our overall conclusion on intangible assets can be summarized as follows. It is an area fraught with difficult conceptual and implementation problems, and we do not have a monopolistic position with respect to their solutions. We believe, however, that financial reporting can be modified so as at least to recognize more of the economic reality of intangible assets than it does now. We recommend the following:

1. Assets and liabilities should be recognized for the present values of future cash flows when (a) they are the result of contractual arrangements and (b) the value thus revealed differs significantly from the cost of subsequent contractual performance (providing the service).

2. The costs associated with stock compensation should be recognized and, if practicable, be measured as an operating expense of the enterprise.

3. Goodwill should not be recognized except briefly as it is determined by the exchange price for an entire enterprise because (a) its determination (except at the rarely-encountered moment of an exchange) is the stuff of financial analysis, not accounting, and (b) its value at that moment is fleeting and has no necessary or causal relationship to its value in the future.

4. Reserve recognition accounting should be reconsidered, supported by adequate prior research.

5. Past cash flows are extremely important and should be reported in terms of (a) their source, (b) the likelihood of their continuance, and (c) the means to replace them when it becomes necessary.

## Financial Statement Dissemination

Financial analysis thrives on information. There is a discussion earlier in this report of the various information sources employed by financial analysts and investment managers. For capital allocation to proceed efficiently in our economy, information must be disseminated both *promptly* and *publicly*. This applies to financial information, both in the form of financial statements and otherwise, as well as to sources of all nonfinancial data that can affect perceptions of the value of companies. The two conditions, promptly and publicly, are complementary. As we explain below, if financial information is not disclosed to the public promptly, it will become known first to a small number of privileged "insiders," only later filtering down to the public at large. Those circumstances place an onerous burden on AIMR members, all of whom are prohibited from using material nonpublic information by the AIMR Code of Ethics and Standards of Professional Conduct.[10]

The economic affairs of an enterprise should be reported in financial statement form at regular and frequent intervals. A year or six months is too long to wait for facts, either good or bad, to be disclosed formally. Less than three months is too short a period for most businesses to make meaningful measurements of economic activity; it also would require excessive periodic assessments of financial status. Thus quarterly interim reporting satisfies optimally the tradeoff between the maximum length of time an analyst should have to wait to receive a report on an enterprise's economic status and the minimum period of time for which meaningful financial measures can be made.

Our comments on quarterly reporting herein have two different purposes. First, we wish to make clear and emphatic our unanimous opposition to recent movements by certain individuals and organizations to abolish mandatory quarterly reporting. Our case takes two forms: (1) substantiating the reasons why quarterly reports are vital to analysts and, perforce, for the efficient functioning of the capital markets, and (2) showing why the arguments made for the eradication of mandated quarterly reporting are specious.[11] Second, we wish to explicate how quarterly financial reporting needs to and should be improved.

---

[10]Section II. C. of the Code of Ethics reads, "The financial analyst shall comply with all laws and regulations relating to the use and communication of material nonpublic information. The financial analyst's duty is generally defined as to not trade while in possession of, nor communicate, nonmaterial nonpublic information in breach of a duty, or if the information is misappropriated.

"Duties under the standard include the following: (1) If the analyst acquires such information as a result of-a special or confidential relationship with the issuer or others, he shall not communicate the information (other than within the relationship), or take investment action on the basis of such information, if it violates the relationship. (2) If the analyst is not in a special or confidential relationship with the issuer or others, he shall not communicate or act on material nonpublic information if he knows, or should have known, that such information (a) was disclosed to him, or would result in a breach of duty, or (b) was misappropriated.

"If such breach of duty exists, the analyst shall make reasonable efforts to achieve public dissemination of such information."

[11]The discussion of quarterly reporting in this paper is necessarily limited. For a more comprehensive presentation of analysts' views on the subject, see the following publication of AIMR's FAPC: Donald Korn, CFA, *The Need for Quarterly Financial Reports from Publicly Owned Companies: A Response to the Competitiveness Debate.* AIMR, 5 Boar's Head Lane, Charlottesville, Virginia 22903 (forthcoming).

**Arguments Supporting Mandated Quarterly Reporting.** The most overwhelmingly important ground for retaining quarterly reporting requirements is that alluded to above, the efficient allocation of capital within the economy. To repeat, financial analysis thrives on information. The more quickly it is made available, the faster investment decisions may be made to direct capital to uses that will maximize overall economic welfare. The ideal state is one in which economic events and their consequences are made public as they occur. In fact, most significant economic events become public knowledge before they are reported in financial statements. Their consequences, however, are a matter of speculation and disagreement among analysts—much of it reasonable and rational, but speculation nonetheless—until financial statements are released. Until that time, uncertainty exists, carrying with it a concomitant increase in capital cost.

Most economic events affecting business enterprises are individually small in relation to the overall economic progress and status of the firm. But they aggregate into numbers of material size. Quarterly reports are the early warning system of the investment world. Some persons have likened them to the mile markers on superhighways. Even though they are not as precise in measurement as mile markers, they at least tell us in what direction the enterprise is going and roughly how quickly it is proceeding.

To analysts, quarterly reports are not only indicators of progress and status to date, they also are important resources for projecting the future. A good part of a financial analyst's work involves making recommendations or engaging in transactions based on expectations of future economic performance. Many analysts are called upon to make formal and frequent estimates of future corporate earnings. Quarterly reports are vital, not as much for what they tell us about the past as to what they tell us about revising our expectations of the future. When a quarterly report contains a "surprise," there usually is an immediate reaction in that enterprise's stock price. The stock price change reflects a change in value not because the past turned out differently than expected but because the market has promptly and alertly changed its expectations of the future.

Deterrence of trading on privileged information is the second major argument in favor of mandated quarterly reporting. As noted above, the code of ethics by which AIMR members work prohibits us from trading on material nonpublic information, and we pride ourselves on our observance of it. Adherence to that code is facilitated by the frequency with which information is made public. If information is withheld from the public by law, it still will be disseminated. The process will be slower, and it will trickle down to the public through a host of privileged insiders and other informed persons who realistically could not be expected to refrain from trading on what they know and others do not. Any attempt to abolish mandated quarterly reporting might better be termed an effort to promote insider trading.

Quarterly reports may be even more important to individual investors than they are to investment professionals. We have a large variety of public sources of information, and we rely on them to confirm in an organized manner our judgments and the fragmentary data on which they are based. For individual investors, public reports may well be and usually are their only source of reliable information. Those who choose to invest in free enterprise should not be denied the information to make those investments in the wisest and best informed manner, not only in their own self-interest but also with the result of improving economic society as a whole.

**Rebuttal of Assertions Against Quarterly Reporting.** Much has been written about the evils of "short-termism" and its impact on management behavior. It is true sometimes that too much emphasis is placed on quarterly earnings reports. It is remarkable that some seemingly sensible people will make decisions based on insignificant deviations from expected earnings. On the other hand, it is quite appropriate for decision makers to revise their forecasts of the future based on new and recent information about the past. The point is that stock prices reflect expectations of the future only, and that past events do not change stock prices as such; they only change expectations. Too many companies have explicitly or implicitly promised consistent quarterly earnings gains; in return, they have received premium price-earnings ratios. The need to achieve target earnings may result in inefficient management practices; in extreme cases, it can result in accounting manipulation or even fraud. As long as a business enterprise keeps its investors informed of its strategies and plans, it has no reason to fear that its share price will suffer for devoting its resources to projects that promise high levels of long-term profitability. Those who contend otherwise either misunderstand or are misrepresenting the functioning of the investment community.

Investors are not only every bit as interested in long-term results as business managers are, but probably even more so. Consider the respective sources of rewards to investment managers and business managements. Investment managers are rewarded for overall performance of investments vis-a-vis the market as a whole. Stock prices, as we have explained at length, are a direct function of expectations of long-run future cash flows. Stock prices do not change because of quarterly past events; they change because of changes in long-run expectations of future events. By contrast, consider how many senior managers are compensated or otherwise rewarded for short-term performance, frequently measured by accounting numbers.

As we stated earlier, "short termism" might better be dealt with by changes in the manner of corporate governance and executive compensation schemes, rather than by eradicating quarterly financial reporting, one of the most vital ingredients in rational and efficient capital allocation. Our system of continuous disclosure helps make markets efficient. Annual earnings have been shown to have limited effect on market prices; three quarterly earnings reports have taken out much of the surprise element. Reduced frequency of reporting would be likely to increase the volatility of securities prices around the time of earnings reports.

Another argument against quarterly reporting is that in most other countries, only semi-annual reports are required or traditional. Some persons believe that reporting requirements in the United States, of which mandated quarterly filings are only one, prevent foreign companies from listing their shares on exchanges here. They prophesy that the United States has lost and will continue to lose stature among the world's capital markets.

We disagree. No foreign company is *prevented* by quarterly reporting requirements from listing its shares here, although some may *elect* not to do so. Many foreign companies are registered in the United States and we cite, from among European companies, the exemplary conduct of Royal Dutch Petroleum Company. It has an active financial relations program in the United States, and its quarterly earnings releases contain detail far beyond British, Dutch, International Accounting Standards Committee (IASC), or even U.S. requirements. The recent decision of Daimler-Benz to be the first German company to provide the disclosures necessary to be listed on the New York Stock Exchange is expected to stimulate a number of other major foreign enterprises to follow suit. As long as capital exists, those who need it will seek it out.

The United States has the most highly developed and sophisticated systems of capital market regulation in the world. The SEC has an admirable record in endeavoring to protect investors, not from the consequences of their own actions but from those who would take unfair advantage of them. The disclosure rules in general, and mandated quarterly reporting in particular, are an integral part of the system to protect investors and the free enterprise system itself. We must be vigilant against those who would subvert that system into promotion of particular market places. Markets exist to serve investors, not the reverse.

**Quarterly Segment Reporting.** The topic of disaggregation is sufficiently important to merit its own separate discussion in the next part of this report. Here we wish to discuss only the need for disaggregated information to be provided more frequently than it is currently. Quarterly segment reporting is a topic that has been advocated by analysts so consistently and so avidly over so many years that it has acquired its own acronym, QSR. In 1990, the FAPC surveyed member analysts in the United States and Canada; they responded overwhelmingly in favor of mandated quarterly segment reporting.[12] Not only do analysts need financial reports as frequently as every three months, they need them in vastly more detail than is mandated today. Some companies do an excellent job in presenting segment data; others offer only the bare minimum disclosures required. We seek a much higher standard to apply to the latter.

It is the unusual publicly owned company that today operates with a single line of business or in a single geographical area. All others require analysis of their separate parts before an assessment can be made of their value as a whole. It is absolutely necessary for analysts not to have to wait for a full year to discover, for example, that a manufacturer of heavy equipment suffered major losses in Latin America earlier in the year. Or that a manufacturing operation has been losing money, a fact concealed by the excessively good results of its finance operations. These data *must* be made available more frequently than is required now.

**Integral versus Discrete Approach to Interim Reporting.**[13] In 1973, Accounting Principles Board Opinion No. 28 (APBO 28) mandated the integral approach to reporting quarterly earnings. Under that opinion, the accounting period is defined as being one year, and quarterly periods are to be regarded as "integral" segments of the annual period. The effect of that standard is to allow the allocation of period costs across interim periods on the basis of benefits received, time elapsed, or other even more arbitrary bases. The result has been allocation that in actuality has ranged from smoothing into outright manipulation of quarterly earnings. Expenses, such as advertising, research, maintenance, income taxes, and so on, are reported discretely year by year. Yet on a quarterly basis, they are unabashedly smoothed and often in ways that appear dubious.

---

[12]A summary of the survey results may be obtained by requesting it in writing from AIMR, 5 Boar's Head Lane, Charlottesville, Virginia 22903.

[13]Our comments on this topic apply only to external financial reporting. There are good and proper reasons why seasonal cost allocation should be followed for product cost determination and other *internal* accounting purposes.

In its early years, the FASB placed on its agenda a reconsideration of APBO 28. The FAPC submitted comments strongly supporting the discrete method. But the project was removed from the FASB's agenda and APBO 28 continues to prevail. We believe that financial analysis is best served by financial reporting that reports transactions as and when they occur. If there is smoothing to be done, it is the province of analysts to do it. If there are financial reporting anomalies that are attributable to seasonality, it is far better to report and explain them than to conceal them with undocumented smoothing. Thus, we recommend changing interim reporting from the integral to the discrete method.

**Auditor Involvement.** The shorter the period of time covered by financial statements, the lower the need for auditor involvement. The need for timeliness is inversely related to the length of the reporting period, and relatively imprecise short-period measurements are difficult to verify. With periods as short as three months, there seems to be little value to be added from auditor involvement with the financial reporting process. In fact, such involvement is likely to diminish timeliness, a primary attribute of interim reports. If external auditors are to be involved, their role should be to assist enterprises to establish procedures and routines that minimize the time taken to get reports prepared and lessen the probability of material errors or misstatements.

In fact, we believe new consideration ought to be given to the audit process and function. One of the comments we received on the exposure draft of this report makes the point bluntly: ". . . We agree that outside auditors might better spend their time assessing the effectiveness of financial and managerial control systems rather than performing routine audits." We advocate a new and different approach to the periodic audit of financial statements.

First, we advocate the continuous involvement of the auditor in the process that generates the financial information an enterprise disseminates externally. The emphasis is on involvement *in the process* rather than only *with the output or results*. We are particularly concerned that the auditor understand and (at a minimum) evaluate the judgments and estimates that enter into financial reports.

Former SEC Chief Accountant John C. Burton once put forth the notion of an "auditor of record," a firm that would take responsibility for the quality and content of an enterprises's publicly released financial information well beyond the mere annual blessing of management's representations in the form of financial statements.

Second, we envision external auditors being substantially more involved than at present with the functioning of the internal systems that produce financial data for external consumption. That involvement could well make more effective use than at present of internal audit and control staff and procedures. In short, we believe that too much attention at present is paid to the numbers and too little to the process that produces them.

We would expect our recommendations, if followed, to have the following results. Audit costs may increase or decrease, but the risk of audit failures would decrease. We expect that even if audit cost were to increase, it would be partially or wholly offset by the decreased cost of capital resulting from higher quality and more reliable information being made available to the financial markets. We also envision instances in which much of the increase in audit activity could be provided by an internal audit team elevated in size and status.

## Disaggregated Financial Statements

Financial analysts have consistently over the years requested financial statement data disaggregated to a much greater degree than it is now. Most analysts have found the provisions of Financial Accounting Standard No. 14, "Financial Reporting for Segments of a Business Enterprise," (FAS 14, issued in 1976), helpful but inadequate. This situation has been exacerbated by the issuance in 1987 of Financial Accounting Standard No. 94, "Consolidation of All Majority-Owned Subsidiaries" (FAS 94). That statement has the good effect of presenting an overall report on complex economic entities and brings onto the consolidated balance sheet a large amount of debt that previously had not appeared there. Its cost has been the loss of much detailed information about subsidiary operations different in character from those of the parent company.

In our previous discussion of quarterly segment reporting, we alluded to the needs of analysts for disaggregated financial data. That need is more than "necessary." It is vital, essential, fundamental, indispensable, and integral to the investment analysis process. Analysts need to know and understand how the various components of a multifaceted enterprise behave economically. One weak member of the group is analogous to a section of blight on a piece of fruit; it has the potential to spread rot over the entirety. Even in the absence of weakness, different segments will generate dissimilar streams of cash flows to which are attached disparate risks and which bring about unique values. Thus, without disaggregation, there is no sensible way to predict the overall amounts, timing, or risks of a complete enterprise's future cash flows. There is little dispute over the analytic usefulness of disaggregated financial data.

There is, however, much controversy over how disaggregated data should be reported. Should it be classified by legal entity, line of business, geographic area, type of customer served, activity (manufacturing, marketing, etc.), Standard Industrial Code number, or any one of many other possibilities? In what degree of detail should it be presented? How extensive can detailed disclosures be made before financial statement users are so overcome with minutia that they not only cannot comprehend them, but they also lose sight of the overall portrayal of the enterprise?

**Reporting How the Business is Managed.** FAS 14 requires disclosure of line-of-business information classified by "industry segment." Its definition of segment is necessarily imprecise, recognizing that there are numerous practical problems in applying that definition to different business entities operating under disparate circumstances. That weakness in FAS 14 has been exploited by many enterprises to suit their own financial reporting purposes. As a result, we have seen one of the ten largest firms in the country report all of its operations as being in a single, very broadly defined industry segment. At the other extreme, there is a publicly owned provider of funeral services that reports in three segments: funeral services, caskets and other merchandise sales, and cemetery operations. We also are aware of and sympathetic with the problems some enterprises have in collecting and reporting data that conform to FAS 14 categories because their businesses are organized and managed differently.

In an ideal world, an enterprise would report disaggregated data in a format that coincides with and reflects how it is organized and managed. It also would disclose the source and nature of risks that are expected to affect, either positively or negatively, the amounts and timing of its future cash flows. These risks may be associated with geography, product lines, markets, or a variety of other classifications. The enterprise would reveal the boundaries between its assorted legal-entity constituents, thus divulging restrictions on the claims of creditors and movements of cash within the entity. Finally, all the disaggregated data disclosed would mirror the way the business is organized and managed, while at the same time providing comparability to the disaggregated data of other enterprises.

In the real world, of course, not all of these objectives can be achieved. They require trade-offs and choices. From the standpoint of financial analysis, we believe priority should be given to the production and dissemination of financial data that reflects and reports sensibly the operations of specific enterprises. If we could obtain reports showing the details of how an individual business firm is organized and managed, we would assume more responsibility for making meaningful comparisons of those data to the unlike data of other firms that conduct their business differently. We realize the extraordinary difficulty of mandating a disclosure standard while maintaining the flexibility of each enterprise to present its own circumstances and organization, but we believe it to be a commendable undertaking.

**Research in Progress and Prognosis for Change.** The topic of disaggregated information is so important to AIMR that it provided the FASB partial funding to support an important research project published in 1992, "Disclosure of Disaggregated Information." This study was followed in May 1993 by an Invitation to Comment, "Reporting Disaggregated Information by Business Enterprises," in which the views of all parties, including those of financial analysts, are sought on a variety of specific issues pertaining to disaggregation.

We commend the FASB for the pace at which the disaggregation project is now moving. It sometimes seems as if the projects that promise to produce information of greatest use to financial analysts are the most interminable. There is no reason for delay or procrastination in giving attention to this subject by (1) standard setters, the FASB, and the International Accounting Standards Committee; (2) capital market regulators, the SEC, and the International Organization of Securities Commissions; and (3) the accounting profession, the AICPA, and the International Federation of Accountants.

**Consolidating Financial Statements.** Although we support the requirement that consolidated financial statements be the basis for general purpose financial reporting, we lament the concomitant loss of detailed information about an economic enterprise's constituent corporate entity components. Currently, published summary data on consolidated subsidiaries are insufficient for analysts to be able to deconsolidate them with sufficient assurance of accuracy. We seek the best of all worlds: *consolidating financial statements*, showing separately the major corporate entities comprised by the whole. Complex entities often prepare these for use by lenders. Since the issuance of FAS 94, a small number of companies have even included them in their published financial reports. There seems to be little reason why they could not be required of all companies. The cost to prepare them would be trivial, except perhaps for additional audit fees caused by a lower materiality threshold. We urge the FASB to consider requiring them.

## Income and Cash Flow Statements

Over the span of the FASB's existence, its pronouncements have become more oriented to the statement of financial position. This is meant as an observation, not criticism.

Perhaps the most apt example is Financial Accounting Standard No. 109, "Accounting for Income Taxes" (FAS 109). It fixes its attention on identifying at a point in time those transactions and events that are deemed to have future tax consequences, then measuring the effect on financial position of the benefits and obligations resulting from them. Their effect on periodic income is calculated only as the necessary consequence of those financial position assessments. This is an approach opposite from the now-superseded Accounting Principles Board Opinion No. 11 (APBO 11), in which the objective was to measure the deferred portion of the current period's provision for income taxes, with resultant balance sheet residuals called deferred tax liabilities and/or assets.

We applaud the efforts and accomplishments of the FASB in making balance sheet amounts more meaningful than before. Prior to FAS 109—and its short-lived predecessor, Financial Accounting Standard No. 96 (FAS 96), deferred tax accounts on the balance sheet had little meaning, because they were remnants of past income statements; today, they depict amounts that an enterprise expects to result in future cash flows. However, as FAS 109 and various other standards have been promulgated, we feel that the development of the income statement has been neglected. We also feel as if more could be done to make cash flow statements more accurate and more useful to analysts. The purpose of this section is to summarize our views on those matters with respect to (1) the income statement, primarily to summarize information scattered throughout earlier parts of this report, and (2) cash flow statements to introduce new material.

**Comprehensive Income.** The FASB's Statement of Financial Accounting Concepts No. 6, "Elements of Financial Statements," paragraph 70, defines comprehensive income as follows:

> Comprehensive income is the change in the equity of a business enterprise during a period from transactions and other events and circumstances from nonowner sources. It includes all changes in equity during a period except those resulting from investments by owners and distributions to owners.

We refer to comprehensive income several times above and have urged the FASB to construct the bridge from concept to standard. It is needed for better and more useful financial reporting in several areas.

First is reporting the impact of changing market values and their effect on the wealth of the enterprise. One of the primary obstacles to acceptance of mark-to-market accounting is how it would magnify the volatility of reported earnings. If both unrealized and realized changes in market value could be revealed for what they are, separately from the results of operating activities, we as analysts would have more information than we do currently, and we might avoid the stock market palpitations that frequently occur because of the information content of a single aggregated number called net income or earnings per share.

Second is to have the goodwill write-off appear as a component of income separate from the operating activities of the enterprise. Earlier, we suggested that goodwill should be written off at the time it is acquired; we did not opine as to whether the write-off should appear on the income statement or go directly to owners' equity. If the concept of comprehensive income were developed, we would expect the write-off to appear separate from the operating activities.

There are other reasons supporting development of the concept of comprehensive income. The FAPC has consistently supported the all-inclusive income statement format, known colloquially as the "clean surplus" approach. We consider income to include all of an enterprise's wealth changes except those engendered from transactions with its owners. We have profound misgivings about the increasing number of wealth changes that elude disclosure on the income statement. Yet individual items may be interpreted differently. That calls for a display of comprehensive income that allows components of different character to be seen and evaluated separately. Some examples follow.

■　　*Unrealized losses on portfolio of marketable securities held for sale.* FAS 115 requires the cumulative net unrealized loss on marketable securities held for sale to be reported directly and separately in the owners' equity section of the balance sheet. That treatment has the effect of reporting the portfolio on the balance sheet at market value  but recognizing gain and loss on the income statement strictly on the cost basis of valuation. There seems to be no conceptual basis for such accounting, nor does it serve well the interests of financial statement users. We consider unrealized security gains and losses to be different in character from realized ones, however, and even more so from other corporate operating activities. Such gains and losses should be included in comprehensive income but displayed in such a manner so that they may be evaluated on their own. This is an important matter to be considered by the FASB, the IASC, other standard-setting bodies, and the SEC as they propel corporate reporting ever nearer to mark-to-market accounting.

■ *Accumulated net gain or loss from the translation of foreign currencies.* Financial Accounting Standard No. 52 (FAS 52) changed the criteria and methodology for the translation of foreign currency and at the same time mandated that the gain or loss from using the current rate method of translation bypass the income statement until such time as the foreign operation was wholly or partially disposed of. We must observe that these are not *true* gains and losses. They are merely the amounts by which the balance sheet is thrown out of balance because the assets and liabilities of a foreign operation are translated at the current rate, but the owners' equity accounts are not. Although it is difficult to visualize those gains and losses as legitimate components of *income*, under the translation methodology specified by FAS 52, we have no other choice.[14]

■ *Unusual and nonrecurring items, restructuring charges, and similar items.* This classification could be broadened well beyond the current category of extraordinary items. It also should be presented in some detail. Some of the items in this group are now presented as extraordinary and shown net of tax. Others are set out as separate line items in income from continuing operations. Still others, such as the effect of lifo liquidations, are ascertainable only by scrutinizing the footnotes. Individual companies tend to have idiosyncratic definitions of what is unusual or nonrecurring as well as eccentric thresholds of materiality. Analysts often are confounded by all of this as they attempt to make comparisons between and among companies, particularly over a time span of several years.

The above list is not exhaustive, but it should be sufficient to support our case. We have not suggested the form or content one or more standards on this subject should take. That is a task for the standard-setters themselves. Our more modest objective merely is to establish the compelling need for attention to this topic. Financial statement users need in one place all the data reporting an enterprise's economic activity, which they then may sort out to suit their own purposes. The resulting income statement format needs codification of its structure to ensure that like items are classified similarly by different

---

[14]We note here the lack of conceptual basis for the current rate method. Furthermore, it does not provide information useful in analysis because of its untoward characteristic of producing accounting numbers that resist interpretation. Although we did not strongly oppose the issuance of FAS 52, we wish to make our current feelings known. Nevertheless, important as that matter is, it is not directly relevant to the point we are making here about comprehensive income.

companies. Only then will analysts be able with increased confidence to make many of the comparisons so vital to their work.

**The Statement of Cash Flows.** Many financial analysts have mixed feelings about Financial Accounting Standard No. 95, "Statement of Cash Flows" (FAS 95). We are gratified that it was issued, because it mandates that a cash flow statement be included in a complete set of financial statements and because it codifies the form and content of that statement. FAS 95 brought to a welcome demise the old statement of changes in financial position, and it eliminated many of the variations in practice among companies that did publish cash flow statements.

Since the issuance of FAS 95, the cash flow statements that have appeared in published financial reports have been much less useful in analysis than we might have expected. First, almost no public company presents its cash flows from operations using the direct format; virtually all use the indirect format. We have learned since the issuance of FAS 95 that it is extremely difficult or impossible in most cases for financial statement users to calculate reasonable estimates of gross operating cash flows (direct method) using only the data provided in financial reports in the indirect format.[15] A second deficiency is the imprecision with which FAS 95 appears to be applied. There is need of an authoritative literature to resolve a variety of ambiguous situations as well as to forestall the many detectable errors we have encountered in published cash flow statements since FAS 95 was issued. We can only speculate on the number of undetectable errors that must also occur.

**The Direct Method of Reporting Cash Flow from Operations.** F A S 95 states, in paragraph 27, "In reporting cash flows from operating activities, enterprises are encouraged to report major classes of gross cash receipts and gross cash payments and their arithmetic sum—the net cash flow from operating activities (the direct method)."

Exposure Draft 36 of the International Accounting Standards Committee Proposed Statement "Cash Flow Statements" states, in paragraph 23, "Enterprises are encouraged to report cash flows from operating activities using the direct method."

Both standard-setting bodies cite the direct method as the preferred method of presenting cash flows from operations. Investment professionals

---

[15]For that reason, we made clear our position that only the direct method should be allowed in our comments to the IASC in letters dated July 25, 1990 re. "Statement of Principles—Cash Flow Statements" and January 20, 1992 re. "E36—Proposed Statement of International Accounting Standards, Cash Flow Statements."

represented by AIMR have expressed their desire for the direct method. We note that Robert Morris Associates, representing more than 15,000 bank loan and credit officers in the United States, has adamantly advocated the direct method.[16] Despite these overwhelming expressions of support for the direct method by virtually all professional users of financial statements in the United States and Canada, it is the indirect method that appears almost without exception in published financial reports.

Two contradictory reasons are given to support the indirect method over the direct. First, it is asserted by some that the specific items used in the indirect method to reconcile income to net cash flow from operations can easily be evaluated by an analyst as to the individual revenues and expenses to which they apply. It is said that the revenues can then be adjusted to determine gross cash collected, the expenses to compute gross cash outflows. Second, it is asserted by many reporting firms that they do not keep their records in such a way as to permit reporting operating cash flows in gross amounts, thereby making the direct method prohibitively expensive to implement.

With respect to the first argument, as a practical matter, there seldom is sufficient detail given in published financial statements of the individual reconciling items to make the adjustments suggested. More often than not, a multitude of individual items appear in the operating section of the cash flow statement as a single number described as "Other," "Other assets and liabilities—net," "Other noncash credits," "Other, net," "Other adjustments—net," etc. In many cases, the level of detail presented in an enterprise's income statement is inconsistent with that in the cash flow statement, and it is consequently impossible to make all of the necessary adjustments. Finally, if the reconciling items "can easily be evaluated by an analyst," they can even more easily (and accurately) be evaluated by the reporting enterprise. Not only that, but evaluation and adjustment, if done by the reporting enterprise, need be done only once, thus saving the greater efforts of and lesser accomplishments by the scores of individual analysts who may follow that firm.

The second argument, professing the high cost of preparing direct format cash flow statements, also is unpersuasive. First, it directly contradicts the first argument, that conversion from direct to indirect is easy, even by analysts relying only on publicly available data. Second, one must ask who bears the costs of preparing financial statements. The costs are paid out of general corporate funds and, ultimately, are borne by the firm's investors—that is, the

---

[16]Robert Morris Associates' position is set forth in public letters to the FASB dated April 21, 1986; September 27, 1986; February 17, 1987; July 14, 1987; and January 5, 1989.

users of financial statements. If financial statement users demand information in a particular form, then it should be provided. If the costs of providing such information truly are prohibitive, the demand will cease as investors refuse to absorb the concomitant decrease in the value of the securities they hold.

A reasonable solution to this apparent impasse is not unattainable. Although the FASB has not seen fit to mandate the direct method, and neither has the IASC, both endorse it as the preferable method. Nothing other than inertia prevents progressive business enterprises that seek favor with analysts from adopting the direct method. We reiterate: Not only is the direct method permitted, users of financial statements prefer it. As professional associations representing financial statement preparers and their auditors consider how they may better provide information that is.valuable to financial statement readers, they should take it upon themselves to champion the direct method of reporting cash flow from operating activities.

**Need for an Authoritative Literature on Cash Flow.**   The need for such a body of authoritative literature manifests itself in two ways. First, there are a variety of accounting matters in which the correct treatment on a cash flow statement is not readily apparent. Inasmuch as cash flow is factual, totally exchange-based, and devoid of allocations, these are entirely questions of classification. Some examples:

■    *Accounting Principles Board Opinion No. 30 specifies that the income statement shall present discontinued operations separately from continuing operations and sets up appropriate definitions and procedures.*[17]   It is unclear from FAS 95 whether cash flows from operating activities should similarly be classified into two distinct components. If the response is affirmative, to what extent and how should taxes paid be allocated between the components of operating activity on the cash flow statement? This question is similar to that of intraperiod tax allocation on the income statement.

■    *FAS 94 requires the consolidation of all majority-owned companies.* Many of these are finance and insurance subsidiaries. Some are integral parts of the parent enterprise's operating activities, others finance and insure primarily unrelated customers, and still others are a blend. To what extent, and following what criteria, are the cash flows related to their receivables and payables to be treated as part of operating activities, as opposed to flows from investing or financing?

---

[17]Recent research has suggested that these definitions and procedures are insufficient to prevent biased applications of them. See Donna Rapaccioli and Allen Schiff, "Reporting Sales of Segments Under APB Opinion No. 30", *Accounting Horizons*, December 1991, pp. 53–9.

■   *Certain enterprises manufacture products that may either be sold or converted to use as plant assets of the enterprise itself.* Examples include certain real estate developments and computers that may be either rented (via operating leases) or sold. How is the cash spent to produce these items to be classified (operating or investing) when the enterprise itself does not know their final disposition until after they have been produced?

There are many other similar questions of classification, but we wish only to illustrate the nature of our concerns.

The second need for authoritative literature is as a bulwark against the myriad errors we have seen in published cash flow statements. We can only speculate about whether they are the result of ignorance, thoughtlessness, or carelessness. The following examples are illustrative.[18]

1. One firm showed as a cash outflow from financing activities the total amount of $30,197 of dividends declared. The $325 increase in its dividends payable account was added to net income in the computation of cash flow from operations.

2. Another corporation included among its investing cash outflows for capital expenditures (and among its financing cash inflows from long-term borrowing) the amounts of assets and liabilities recorded at the inception of capital leases during the year.

3. Several companies show bank overdrafts as current liabilities on their balance sheets. These companies then place the amount of the change in that liability on the cash flow statement as an adjustment of income in the calculation of cash flow from operations. That treatment is tantamount to making the cash flow statement directly contradictory to the balance sheet. The balance sheet asserts that payments have been made by overdrawing a bank account; the cash flow statement asserts that the payments were not made. One of those statements has to be false and misleading.

4. A firm states in the notes to its financial statements that it "acquired 168 businesses, all of them accounted for as purchases, for $303,601,000 in cash and notes." The cash flow statement shows a cash payment of $303,601,000. The amount paid for with notes should not have been reported on the cash flow statement; it should have appeared as supplementary data.

5. That same firm shows an increase in its "Investment in a less-than-majority-owned affiliate" from a beginning balance of zero to an ending balance of $249,718. The firm's cash flow statement shows a

---

[18]Because errors of the type we cite are so frequently encountered in published cash flow statements, we see no point in naming and possibly embarrassing the individual companies responsible for the examples cited below.

deduction from net income for $5,017 of equity earnings from the investment; yet the supplementary data state that the cost of the investment in the affiliate (none paid in cash) was $249,718.

6. A third violation by that same firm is its deduction from income in computing cash flow from operations of an *after-tax* gain of $11,354 recognized from certain nonmonetary transactions, even though the gain was properly reported on the income statement in its *pre-tax* amount.

The solution to the sorts of problems listed above is two-faceted. First is the need for detailed procedural guidance to the preparation of cash flow statements well beyond that incorporated in intermediate accounting textbooks. Second, both the preparers and auditors of financial statements need to educate their personnel. We deliberately use the word "education," not "training." We believe that instruction in procedural matters is secondary to an understanding of the role of the statement of cash flows as a major financial statement and the philosophy of its system of classification into operations, investing, and financing. We suspect that in practice it frequently is prepared in haste as a derivative of the audited balance sheet and income statement without due consideration for its unique and eminent position among the major financial statements.

## Transition to New Standards

Fundamental analysts use data bases of one sort or another. The data bases may be commercial in origin or they may be assembled by the analysts themselves. They may be accessed electronically or they may be in hard copy form. They may be extensive or limited in scope. The point is that they are used to make comparisons between and among firms and over time periods several years in length. The validity of those data bases may be enhanced in one sense—but certainly impaired in another—each time a new accounting standard is issued. As some or all enterprises adopt the new standard, it ought to have the effect of improving interfirm comparisons by eliminating differences attributable only to accounting. But it is certain to destroy the continuity of previous periods' accounting numbers with those of the present and future.

It should be apparent that AIMR does not oppose the issuance of new accounting standards. Indeed, much of this report is devoted to suggesting changes that we feel would improve the usefulness of financial reports. Our objective in this section is to advocate methods of transition to new standards that would precipitate minimum disruption to the continuity of data analysts use.

We have sincere reservations about the transition methods and procedures specified by FASB pronouncements issued in recent years. Perhaps the epitome of our concern came with the issuance of Statement of FAS 96 in 1987, followed by FAS 100 in 1988, FAS 103 in 1989, FAS 108 in 1991, and FAS 109 in 1992. FAS 96, which set new standards for reporting income taxes in financial statements, permitted two transition methods and a three-year transition period. An enterprise could choose to adopt FAS 96 in 1987, 1988, or 1989. The adopting enterprise could choose to restate as many of its prior years as it wished, or it could choose to place the entire cumulative retroactive effect of the change on the income statement of the year it adopted FAS 96. FAS 100 extended the effective date of FAS 96 from 1989 to 1990; FAS 103 extended it further through 1992; and FAS 108 extended it through 1993. Finally, FAS 96 was superseded by FAS 109, which also has a 1993 effective date and continues the choice of transition methods allowed by FAS 96.

We realize that there were special circumstances attaching to the replacement of FAS 96 by FAS 109, but the impact on analysis was devastating. Starting in 1987 and continuing through 1993, seven full years, we have had to compare companies using up to three different paradigms of accounting for income taxes. Many firms continued to follow the provisions of APBO 11 and persisted in doing so until forced to switch in fiscal year 1993. Others adopted FAS 96 but postponed making the transformation to FAS 109. Still others were early adopters of FAS 109. Furthermore, at the time that firms adopted FAS 109, there still were differences in the disposition of the cumulative effect of the change on prior years' income. Not until 1994, when analysts receive 1993 annual reports, will they have comparable data on income taxes among all firms. And it will be sometime into the 21st century before analysts will have a sufficient number of comparable years of data to do sensible time-series analysis on reported income tax numbers.

If FAS 96 and its successors were an isolated instance, our cause for complaint would be modest. But it is not. FAS 106, "Employers Accounting for Postretirement Benefits Other Than Pensions," has resulted in perhaps the most sizable cumulative adjustments in the history of standards setting. Companies adopting that standard also have been given considerable time (1990–93 for domestic plans: 1990–95 for foreign plans) and a choice of methods (immediate or delayed recognition of the transition amounts). In one way, FAS 106 is much more destructive of data base construction than FAS 96 and its successors. Delayed recognition of the transition amount will extend over 20 years subsequent to adoption of the statement. For enterprises adopting it for domestic plans in 1993, their financial statements may include this vestige of the past until the beginning of fiscal year 2013. It will take an astute and perspicacious financial statement reader to abstract from the footnote data required by FAS 106 the facts necessary to adjust financial statements to be comparable. Those who rely on commercial data bases do not even have the opportunity to make such adjustments.

It seems as if the FASB has tended in recent years towards longer transition periods and more choice on the part of business firms on how to account for mandated changes in accounting principles. We understand that the motivation for such flexibility may well originate from the complexity of certain recent standards as well as the magnitude of their effect on financial statements. From the standpoint of financial analysts, recent relaxation by the FASB of quick and strict transition procedures is untimely. Increased availability and use of electronically accessed financial data bases, with the promise of the SEC's Electronic Data Gathering and Retrieval scheme to be widely available soon, reduces substantially opportunities for analysts to fashion the tedious adjustments necessary to make financial statements comparable. Furthermore, analysts should not need to make such adjustments. Long transition periods and multiple methods may be politically prudent, but they dramatically reduce the usefulness of financial statements.

We would be better served if those who set standards and disclosure rules would designate a *common date* for adoption of a new accounting standard and a *final date* for complying with a new disclosure requirement. We urge those dates to be as soon as feasible after the new rules are promulgated and published. Standard setters and capital market regulators need to gather evidence on that feasibility as part of their normal processes. The collection of evidence needs to go beyond merely hearing the assertions of business enterprises about their anticipated difficulties in applying the prospective rules. As we note below, field testing often can be a vital ingredient in making transition more rapid and productive for all.

Most important of all to financial analysts is the need for a single method. We have observed, without surprise, that the existence of choices has introduced bias into financial reports. Any sensible financial manager, given a choice of methods, must select the one that makes his or her firm look best, if for no other reason than not to appear irrational to those who provide capital to the firm. As a result, we tend to see cumulative effect *credits* appear on current and future-period income statements, while equivalent *debits* go directly to owners' equity. Given the equality of debits and credits, a new debit to the past can only result in equal credit to current or future periods, sometimes revealed and sometimes not.[19]

A transition method that requires a restatement of prior periods to the new accounting principle is generally preferable to alternative methods. Presumably, a change in standards is promulgated to effect improvement. If prior periods' reports can be restated to achieve those same improvements, we will have new information about the past. More importantly, restatement gives financial analysts a head start in constructing a new time-series data base. Restatement starts us off under the new standard with three years of data under the new accounting principle. Our one reservation with respect to restatement is that it is not in accordance with the concept of comprehensive income, which we advocate and promote throughout this report. As a practical matter, however, the comparability attained through restatement for accounting principles changes is more important to most analysts than is strict adherence to our support of comprehensive income.

In some cases, it is impossible or impractical to restate the past for the effect of a newly issued financial accounting standard. Examples that come to mind are changes resulting from the issuance of Financial Accounting Standard No. 34, "Capitalization of Interest Cost"; FAS 52, "Foreign Currency Translation"; Financial Accounting Standard No. 76, "Extinguishment of Debt" (FAS 76); and a variety of amendments and changes to existing accounting standards.[20] In those cases, the cumulative retroactive effect of the change, if it can be computed, should be reported on the current period's income statement separately and with full disclosure. We are unable to perceive conceptual grounds for carrying any such cumulative effect forward and, even worse, using it to smooth the reported incomes of future periods. If the latter procedure is mandated or allowed anyway, its effect on the income of each future period affected not only must be disclosed, it should additionally be

---

[19]We are fascinated by the enterprise that elected early adoption of FAS 96 via restatement, thus reducing its retained earnings by hundreds of millions of dollars of "derecognized" deferred income tax benefits. In subsequent years, that firm's unrecognized deferred tax benefits decreased, thus reducing its income tax provision and increasing its net income. That same firm then elected early adoption of FAS 109, but chose to recognize the cumulative retroactive effect of the change, the recognition of previously "derecognized" tax benefits, as an adjustment of income in the year of the change. As a result, all of the hundreds of millions of deferred tax benefits "derecognized" at January 1, 1987, ended up appearing on the income statement twice. We do not fault the financial managers. They did what they had to do. We do regret the opportunity being available to them.

[20]The fact that we cite FAS 34, FAS 52 and FAS 76 as examples in which restatement would not be advisable is in no way related to the fact that each of these is a standard whose issuance financial analysts believe worsened rather than improved the quality and usefulness of financial reporting.

presented separately from events of the current year or highlighted to point it out clearly to otherwise unsuspecting readers of the financial report.

In some cases, a new standard may be applied only to transactions originating after a specified date, for reasons that either are practical or political. We believe such treatment is justified only in rare cases and carries with it a responsibility on the part of reporting enterprises to inform financial statement users of the extent to which that new standard has affected them as long as there are material amounts carried forward from the past under different accounting.

**A Note on Field Testing.** AIMR's FAPC has on several occasions communicated directly to the FASB its support of field testing in the standard-setting process. Field tests can be enormously helpful in identifying implementation problems that neither preparers nor users of financial statements could have anticipated at the conceptual level. We commend those enterprises and their auditors who have volunteered their time, funds, and efforts to test proposed standards in the past, and we encourage others to participate in the future.

AIMR also is enthusiastic about the prospect of certain financial analysts and other financial statement users participating in field tests. We believe they could add an important and heretofore absent dimension to the testing process. To date, field tests have concentrated on the feasibility of preparer implementation of proposed new accounting methods. Financial statement users would be able to comment on the value of the information generated by those methods. They could also recommend the forms of presentation that would best serve effective dissemination of the information contained in the data. Specifically, they could provide expert opinion as to how well the new methods create knowledge that is useful to the process of valuation.

If investment professionals were to participate in field tests, safeguards would be needed to protect the confidentiality of the information being generated. The first of these is Section II C of the AIMR Code of Ethics.[21] Only AIMR members who would not find field test information useful in their trading or related activities could participate. Eligible testers would include a variety of working analysts as well as other AIMR members, such as academics and others not currently or directly participating in capital market transactions. Additionally, there are undoubtedly many circumstances in which additional practicing analysts could participate without having to know the identity of individual field test firms or (sometimes) their industry affiliation. Finally,

---

[21] See footnote 10.

there would have to be ways to assure the business enterprises participating in field tests that the safeguards were operative and effective.

## The Standard-Setting Process

AIMR has long been an active participant in the standard-setting process, both in the United States and internationally. It has presented its views in writing and in testimony more frequently than any other organization of financial statement users. Anthony T. Cope, former co-chairman of AIMR's Advocacy Steering Committee and long-time FAPC member, was appointed to the FASB for an initial term beginning July 1, 1993. Frank Block, long-time member and former chairman of the FAPC, served one term as a FASB board member. Patricia McConnell, current chairman of the FAPC, is a member of the Board of the International Accounting Standards Committee (IASC) and recently was replaced by Peter C. Lincoln, another FAPC member, on the Financial Accounting Standards Advisory Council that advises the FASB on matters it has currently and prospectively under consideration. Gerald I. White, former long-time chairman of the FAPC, serves on the IASC Advisory Board and frequently presents the views of financial analysts on financial reporting matters. George H. Boyd III currently occupies the "financial analyst chair" as a trustee of the Financial Accounting Foundation, the organization that sponsors and supports the FASB. Financial analysts almost always are represented on task forces organized by the FASB to prepare discussion documents on agenda items. Financial analysts from the United States frequently have served on IASC steering committees (similar to FASB task forces).

With the exception of the two full-time FASB members, all individual analysts cited above serve as volunteers and render their services to the standard-setting process *in addition to*, not as part of, their regular work as analysts, money managers, research directors, academics, etc. Their dedication is commendable. Furthermo e, they have the task of representing, with both time and funding in meager supply, the majority of professional users of financial statements. Their views deserve to be heard, even though they are outnumbered and outspent by the legions of business firms, industry and business policy associations, large auditing firms, and professional associations of accountants, many of which have full-time, paid staffs to research and advocate their views on financial reporting matters.

**National Standard-Setting for Global Financial Markets.** A s d i s -

cussed in some detail earlier in this report, financial markets have transcended national boundaries and the sovereignty of individual states. Accounting standards continue to be promulgated locally with all of the expected chauvinism, conflicts, cultural biases, and other ingredients of heterogeneity. The IASC faces a huge task as it strives to set forth a common set of standards without the authority to enforce adherence to them. Given the degree of disputation in any one country when major new standards are proposed, international disagreement can be expected to be a multiple of that.

We have been favored in the United States and Canada with bodies of accounting standards and financial disclosure requirements that are generally more comprehensive than elsewhere in the world. We also have single sets of accounting standards that, with few exceptions, apply equally to all enterprises, large and small, public and private. Standard-setting generally has been done in the private sector, although not without intensive oversight and occasional supersession by government. In many countries, accounting standards are set by law or government fiat, sometimes by law intended primarily to serve purposes (such as tax assessment) only peripherally related to financial reporting. Some countries set rigid legal requirements for company accounts but allow more flexibility for consolidated financial reports, Japan and France being useful examples. Some countries have written and agreed-upon conceptual frameworks to support their standards; in others, their frameworks are implicit only.

All of these differences, until somehow resolved, have certain deleterious consequences. Until such time as there are universal financial reporting precepts, the risks associated with cross-border financing will remain high. Stock exchange listings will necessarily remain parochial.[22] Transaction costs relating to trades of foreign securities will remain high. These consequences, although expensive, are far less costly than would be the degradation of the integrity and efficiency of the capital allocation process in North America should there be significant reductions in the frequency, quality, or quantity of financial information available now.

We are in somewhat of a quandary as to the best course to take to achieve truly meaningful and generally accepted international accounting standards. Our suggestions here are less forceful than elsewhere in this report. Much of the subsequent discussion of this topic consists of questions, not answers. As

---

[22]AIMR disagrees with William H. Donaldson, President of the New York Stock Exchange. He is portrayed in a *Wall Street Journal* article ("Big Board, SEC Fight Over Foreign Stocks", May 13, 1992, Page C1) as wanting to ". . . persuade the Securities and Exchange Commission to soften strict U.S. rules so that foreign companies with looser financial disclosures can be traded on the Big Board."

we consider the set of steps that can be taken to achieve true international standards, some of the questions that arise are:

- Can a single set of standards be truly compatible with business methods and practices that vary from culture to culture around the world?
- Will competition among national interests cause international standards to be weak or robust? How many alternative choices should be allowed? Will smaller, weaker, less developed countries be able to influence standards setting? How and to what extent?
- What enforcement mechanisms will work? Is the International Organization of Securities Commissions (IOSCO) the proper body to bring compulsion to international standards? What about countries that do not have representation on IOSCO? Are there more appropriate international bodies? Are non-adopters of international standards to be shunned in the capital markets of the world?
- Is the IASC as presently constituted the proper body to formulate international standards? Should the accounting profession, founder of the IASC, be supplanted by some other group such as national standard-setting organizations, thus making the IASC into a supranational standards-setting body?
- How should the views of interested parties be presented to the IASC? Should, for example, each national or regional organization of financial analysts offer its separate opinion, or should analysts worldwide attempt to reach consensus first? The same questions apply to professional accountants and business enterprises.
- Will international standards be accepted by the SEC as an alternative to U.S. standards? Will they be accepted only for foreign companies or for all registrants? If so, what would be the effect on privately owned U.S. companies? Would they also have to follow international GAAP? If not, would a separate set of national accounting standards have to be maintained solely for them?

There are many other unanswered questions. This report is too brief to present all of them or to explore their answers in reasonable depth, especially because so many of them are interrelated. In any event, financial analysts expect to play a major role in formulating answers to them. We are pleased with the extent of our participation on the international scene to date. We plan not only to maintain our presence but to expand it as we continue to approach a world of finance that is truly global.

**The Role of the FASB.** We do not know what the future role of the FASB will be, but at the moment it certainly is the paramount standard-setting organization affecting financial analysis in the United States. Over the years, we have had differences with the FASB, and we have discussed many of them and noted others at various places in this report. Those differences are inevitable given our single-mindedness in seeking information useful in the workings of investment analysis. They in no way subvert our total support of the FASB as an institution. We are on the record[23] in that regard. All of our comments herein are made with the hope of improving its operations, strengthening its perseverance, and raising its stature.

From time to time, the FASB is criticized, disparaged, assailed, censured, and even castigated by various individuals and organizations. Much of that criticism seems to us unwarranted, as we discuss in greater detail below. It seems to be as much an expression of disappointment and disagreement as anything else. In fact, the more we hear of it, the more convinced we are that the FASB is accomplishing its mission. It has undertaken some of the most daunting projects imaginable: financial instruments, post-retirement benefits of all sorts, and reporting income taxes, among others. It has been lobbied incessantly by, among others, the Business Roundtable, various competing government agencies, a variety of financial institution trade associations, and various trade associations and similar groups.

Perhaps the best way to appreciate the virtue of the FASB is to ask who or what could do a better job. The answer is clear. There is no alternative arrangement that would come close to achieving the integrity of the FASB and its ability, by promulgating accounting standards, to compel the propagation of unpopular truth through financial reports. We, in common with others, could hope for standards more beneficial to our needs. Unlike many others, we also encourage the FASB to act more rapidly in considering and issuing standards. We have consistently opposed changes in the board's operating procedures that act to slow its tempo. We hope it is clear that our position is one of thorough support for the institution, without complete endorsement of all its actions or conduct.

**Need for User Viewpoints in Standard-Setting Bodies.** In 1993, for only the second time has the Financial Accounting Foundation appointed to the FASB an individual from the community of professional financial statement users. By contrast, the IASC includes two financial analysts as members of the board and several others on its advisory committee and various steering committees. As a result, financial analysts and investment managers often have felt alienated from the standard-setting process in the United States,

---

[23]See Appendix A, specifically letters dated April 8, 1991, and February 2, 1990.

"the beggar at the feast" as one prominent investment manager stated.[24] We observe FASB members being selected from the ranks of auditing firms, business enterprises, academia, and government. Every realm, save one, seems continuously to provide board members.

Most practicing financial analysts are neither accounting technicians nor theorists. They do not have the time, given the demands of their work and the limited (but vital) role financial reporting plays in it. Some might say that is a reason *not to* appoint financial analysts or other financial statement users to the FASB. But it is more a reason *to* make such selections. First, we must keep in mind that the primary purpose of financial reporting is to provide information that is valuable to financial statement users; it is not merely to produce reports that comply with a variety of arcane requirements nor to provide employment to accountants. Therefore, those who use financial statements should have a major voice in determining their form and content.

Second, financial statement users have perhaps the paltriest resources with which to influence the FASB or otherwise present their views. As we point out above, we feel badly outspent and outnumbered in the "due process" activities of the FASB. The effort that we do expend is with the goodwill and forbearance of generally demanding employers and is dependent on the willingness of individual investment professionals to relinquish a certain amount of their personal or leisure time to further the interests of their fellows.

Third, there is compelling need for members of the FASB to provide a point of view that has been largely absent from the board's inner workings. We are well aware that board members are required to sever all ties with their previous employers and that members are to act in the interests of the board's entire constituency, not as representatives of special interest groups. An investment professional appointed to the board also would have to adhere to those terms and we would expect no less. Still, all persons are the sum of their experiences. It is baffling to us that the Financial Accounting Foundation allowed the FASB to carry on year after year missing the background and experience of at least one financial statement user. We cannot imagine anything more pertinent or germane to the board as it strives to fulfill its mission and put into practice the tenets of its conceptual framework.

**Recent Criticism of the FASB.** The issuance in late 1987 by the FASB of three major pronouncements marked the escalation of previously scattered

---

[24]Gerald I. White, "The Coming Deregulation of Accounting Principles," *Financial Reporting and Standard Setting*, Gary John Previts, Ed. (New York: American Institute of Certified Public Accountants) 1991, p. 35.

protests into more serious dissention. "FASB bashing" became close to sport in some quarters. We agree with some of the opposition, but we differ with the passion (and sometimes vitriol) with which a good deal of it has been expressed. In most cases, we believe that the FASB's critics either are mistaken or are acting in a self-interested manner. Some of the criticisms we have heard, and our answers to them are summarized in the list that follows.

■   *Financial reports have become difficult to understand.* We agree, but for quite different reasons. First, business activity has become more complex. Second, the FASB has had the fortitude to confront difficult problems that are not amenable to simplistic answers. We do not expect the financial affairs of multifarious economic organisms to be reducible to a few simple comprehensive easy-to-read numbers. It just is not possible.

However, we could and do expect a better effort on the part of enterprises issuing financial reports to make their affairs more understandable to the investment analysts and advisors who simply are unable to devote major portions of their time to digesting imposing new pronouncements on abstruse accounting topics. Financial reports have taken on the appearance of compliance documents rather than communication tools. There is no need for that. Some investment analysts have even begun to question whether those who prepare financial reports understand the purpose for which a particular standard was issued. The FASB and the SEC set *minimum* disclosure requirements. There is no proscription on relating more or explaining that which is disclosed. We should not blame the FASB because it cannot mandate a willingness on the part of managements to decipher and illuminate their affairs.

■   *The FASB has issued too many standards too quickly.* The FASB commenced operations in 1973, 20 years before this report was completed. In that interval, it has issued 117 standards and substantially fewer interpretations. The rate is fewer than six standards per year. But the rate of issuance of major new standards with broad impact across all industries is between one and two a year. The vast majority of the FASB's new standards are modifications of existing pronouncements, adoption as standards of existing AICPA literature, or matters that affect specific industries, including not-for-profit enterprises. Not only that, the standards themselves are relatively brief. Most of the bulk is supplied by the included illustrations and practice guides requested by financial statement preparers and their auditors.

Nor can the pace at which major new broad-based standards are issued be characterized as swift. In our comments on transition, we remark on the number of years it takes before a new standard is fully implemented. In addition, many new standards take numerous years from the time they are placed on the FASB's agenda until a final standard is approved by a minimum 5-2 vote, the so-called "super majority." The change a few years ago from a simple majority vote for approval of a new standard to the "super majority" was designed to slow further the board's already glacial pace.

Complaints about too many standards, standards adopted too quickly, or too-complex standards seem to be mistaken but may actually be misdirected. Major new standards are infrequent and, shorn of accompanying material, relatively succinct. However, the numbers and size of the new reading material emanating from the FASB is overwhelming. Most of it pertains to matters in progress. Perhaps if the process were to be speeded up, fewer interim reports of various sorts would be produced, thus lessening the seemingly endless pondering by all of unfinished agenda matters.

■ *The FASB is too theoretical.* This argument is heard frequently but simply is not true. In fact, the FASB in many cases has issued standards that are obviously contrary to good accounting theory. For example:

1. FAS 87 and FAS 106 on employers' accounting for pensions and other postretirement benefits, respectively, contain a variety of procedures and choices that allow smoothing of transition balances, actuarial and experience gains and losses, and the cost or benefit of plan amendments over many accounting periods, thus smoothing the annual pension costs in ways unsupported by accounting theory.

2. FAS 15[25] specifies accounting for restructured debt using methods that ignore the time value of money. FAS 15 directly conflicts with Accounting Principles Board Opinion No. 21, "Interest on Receivables and Payables." One of its effects was to allow financial institutions in the U.S. two different accounting results for optional alternative settlements of the Mexican debt, even though the alternatives were identical *in substance.*

3. FAS 52 provides that assets and liabilities expressed in foreign currency, where the local currency is the functional currency, shall be translated at the exchange rate at the balance sheet date. The result is that real assets (property, inventories, etc.) are treated as if they are money. To prevent obviously absurd results, FAS 52 prohibits application of that method to currencies of highly inflationary[26] economies.

---

[25]FAS 15 was superseded by the issuance in 1993 of FAS 114, but the example of FAS 15 still is instructive. First is the remarkably long time it took for the FASB to replace a seriously deficient standard. Second, we view FAS 114 as an improvement over FAS 15, but we believe it too has aspects that are incongruent with sound accounting theory.

[26]Highly inflationary is defined as a rate of general inflation exceeding 100 percent for the three-year period ending on the balance sheet date.

In our opinion, a more accurate accusation would be that the FASB is not sufficiently theoretical in its pronouncements. We often are disappointed by the issuance of a standard that incorporates one or more flagrant departures from theory seemingly to make it more palatable to other members of the business community. Each departure from theory makes the data contained in financial statements less interpretable or comprehendible only with additional analytic effort.

It is quite possible that those who denounce the FASB for being too theoretical are in actuality complaining less about the standards issued than about the succession of documents that antedate issuance of a standard. Commentators are forced by discussion memoranda, invitations to comment, exposure drafts and the like, to provide conceptually valid support for the positions they take. Respondents therefore are required to be more than familiar with the FASB's conceptual framework project as well as with the greater body of "common law" accounting and economic theory. In addition, they are called upon to be up-to-date on new and seminal conceptual and empirical work, not only in accounting but also in finance and economics. Although their grievances are filed with the FASB, they might be more accurately directed to those persons who are pushing back the frontiers of knowledge.

■ *The cost of applying new standards is excessive.* For something to be excessive, it must exceed the right, proper, or correct amount. Yet there is no reference amount of cost that one can characterize or measure out as being correct. In short, excessiveness is a value judgment. Assertions that it exists do not make it true.

In particular, it is the providers of financial statements from whom the claim of excessive cost is heard. We can respond by asserting that the cost to them, high as it may seem, is still less than the benefit to financial statement users of (1) minimizing the cost of providing the data by having the firm do it once and provide it to multitudes of users who otherwise would individually have to replicate the firm's effort; (2) having the firm as the source of information, thus obviating the need for analysts to scavenge for less reliable data from secondary sources; and (3) making available an additional source of information that confirms or denies other sources. One of the charges to the FASB in its mission statement is "to promulgate standards only when the expected benefits exceed the perceived costs." We wish them well in trying to implement a notion for which there is a paucity of guidance in the literature of welfare economics. We hope they will not succumb to judging the issue based on the quantity and loudness of the voices they hear.

Finally, we need to consider who bears the cost of providing the information that appears in financial reports. In one very real sense, there is no added compliance cost to financial statement preparers. Their salaries remain unchanged and may even be enhanced as the scope of their responsibilities is enlarged. The costs are paid out of general corporate funds and, ultimately, are borne by the firm's investors, the users of financial statements. The cost of information is one of the prices we pay for efficient financial markets. But the benefit of rational capital allocation can be far in excess of the relatively small amounts paid to make financial markets efficient. Investors are the ones who suffer both the cost and reap the benefits of improved financial reports. We would hope that company managers, who are their agents, should not confuse their own personal interests with those of their principals.

■    *The FASB is inimical to the interests of financial statement preparers.* This is a variation on the criticisms already discussed above. It can be addressed briefly. We have seen much concerted action of the part of financial statement preparers, in particular the Business Roundtable, to attempt to stifle the work of the FASB. We view these actions with much trepidation, our concern being that the size of the forces deployed by the critics of FASB might be construed as measuring the justness of their cause.

The cause needs to be examined on its own merits. The discussion of specific complaints immediately above indicates that they have little or no substance. We believe that any declaration to the effect that the FASB does not serve the interests of financial statement preparers is not only wrong, it is self-serving. First, some financial analysts hold the exact opposite view; they feel that the FASB favors preparers. We also find that view self-serving. The fact is that the FASB is not to serve any specific constituent group. It is to serve equally and even-handedly everyone with an interest in financial reporting. That is why the members of the board must sever all ties with their previous employers. As long as *everyone*, financial analysts included, believes that their interests could be better served, the FASB must be doing a good job of balancing competing interests for the good of the whole.

■    *Does the FASB follow due process?* Some commentators have taken the FASB to task for not following due process. Their opinion seems to be. that the FASB should be following the popular view as expressed by the majority of the comments directed to it. In that view, the setting of accounting standards is almost entirely a political process in which lobbying is seen as a productive activity. Our view is quite to the contrary.

First, we believe that the politicization of accounting should be kept to a minimum. It should not be used to serve special interests. The FASB needs information from its various constituencies that will aid it in seeing that important information is provided to financial statement users without causing undue turmoil on the part of preparers. Lobbying is an extreme form of information transmittal that has negligible legitimacy in the standard-setting process. After all, we are speaking of the measurement of economic phenomena; no matter how fine the sentiments expressed, the laws of economics defy change.

Second, we are convinced that, if anything, the FASB is too concerned with due process and sunshine. In many cases, the system has acted to slow almost to a halt the pace at which new standards are issued. The stages seem excruciatingly slow on occasion. Now the FASB has gone to extended comment periods on two recent discussion memoranda.[27] We also suggest that the prohibition on a majority of the board members meeting in private or without advance public notice is unnecessary. In fact, we believe that the quality and quantity of the board's work could improve if some of it at least were sheltered from continual scrutiny.

---

[27]"Consolidation Policies and Procedures," issued September 10, 1991, with a comment deadline of July 15, 1992; and "New Basis Accounting," issued December 18, 1991, with a comment deadline of July 15, 1992.

# SUMMARY OF IMPORTANT POSITIONS
# AND GUIDE TO FUTURE ACTIONS

Much of this report relates to the current state of the art and implications for future developments in financial reporting. Rightfully, so do most of the positions stated in this section. Before presenting them, however, we must note that they all build on positions taken by AIMR in the past. For many years, the AIMR's Corporate Information Committee, SEC Liaison Committee, and Financial Accounting Policy Committee (FAPC) have spoken often and forthrightly in presenting our views and those of our predecessor organizations, the Financial Analysts Federation and the Institute of Chartered Financial Analysts.

The FAPC "maintains contact with both private and public sector accounting groups that establish accounting standards to ensure the needs of investors are communicated and included as standards are promulgated." Its primary activity is to react to initiatives from those bodies. The extent of that activity can be noted from Appendix A, a list of the letters of comment produced and sent by the FAPC over a five-year period ended April 16, 1993. In addition to its comment letters, the FAPC issues broad position papers on financial reporting and accounting matters. It also has sponsored research on accounting matters, the most recent being quarterly segment reporting. It was commissioned by AIMR to write this report.

The SEC Liaison Committee is the subcommittee of the FAPC that takes responsibility for AIMR relations with the SEC. Appendix B contains a list of that committee's communications with the SEC between February 2, 1989, and April 10, 1991. The major work of the Corporate Information Committee is to evaluate the quality of financial reporting and to designate awards to firms that excel in meeting their reporting obligations. Each year, the committee publishes a lengthy report of its findings together with a description of its activities and criteria for selection. Copies of the report are available from AIMR.[1]

We expect the positions set forth below to build on the precedents of the past. That does not prevent them from breaking new ground, but they do not introduce significant inconsistencies with previous AIMR positions. To the

---

[1] The most recent report is 1992–93, although limited quantities from some previous years also are available. Each report is free to AIMR members upon request and may be purchased by others—subject to availability—for $50. To order, please contact the AIMR Publications Sales Department, P.O. Box 7947, Charlottesville, Virginia 22906; telephone 804/980-3647; fax 804/977-0350.

extent that they do establish new stances, it is largely the result of the changing world that we describe earlier in this report.

## Strive for a World-Wide Acceptable GAAP, Including Disclosure Standards

This report discusses at some length the rapid pace of financial market globalization. One of the main impediments to the efficient movement of capital to the places it is best employed is a lack of information that is comparable in either quantity or quality. We support enthusiastically the efforts of the International Accounting Standards Committee, the International Organization of Securities Commissions and others to remove or at least reduce that hindrance.

Our enthusiasm is expressed with an unequivocal caution. We will not consent to a lowering of the standards of disclosure that we currently possess. Investment professionals have been integral constituents in establishing the disclosure system currently in effect. Our criticisms of it notwithstanding, there is none better in the world. Some persons in authority have suggested that it is more important for the United States to conform to a global set of disclosure standards than it is to maintain the level of disclosure that now prevails in the United States. We disagree. Our reasons are discussed in detail elsewhere in this report.

## Set Financial Information in Its Business Context

For financial analysts to make sound judgments and draw rational conclusions, they must judge the performance of individual business enterprises. Performance appraisal is largely a matter of evaluating how well the management of an enterprise has achieved its goals. Businesses are for the most part operated according to plans, either explicit or implicit. Investment professionals aspire to allocate capital to those plans that seem most likely to succeed. To do so, they need information of two types.

First, management should explicitly describe its strategies, plans, and expectations. Much of this must come in the form of narrative descriptive material. Dollar amounts of budgeted and other anticipated amounts are useful for expressing plans in more concrete terms. Goals for growth rates in revenues, market share, and the like should be stated. Analysts need anticipated amounts of key ratios, such as the return on total invested capital or on equity, the ratio of debt to equity, etc. Factors that are expected to affect those ratios—such as major financing or capital spending plans—should be divulged.

Second, results should be reported in a manner that is consistent with the organization and management of the firm. Different entities, even within the same industry, may organize their operations in dissimilar ways. Financial analysts need information in formats that allow them to compare those firms both against each other and against the firms' own business plans. The task of devising accounting and disclosure standards to mandate dissemination of information in the fashion we advocate is perhaps not totally surmountable. Thus we hope business enterprises themselves will act with goodwill and in their own interests to explain themselves and their operations in "user friendly" ways even when it is not required.

## The Role of Current Values in Financial Reports

A great controversy has arisen recently over mark-to-market accounting. Feelings are strong both in favor of it and against it, with a spectrum of opinion in between. Financial analysts also have diverse views, even though they are not as extreme as others may be. Few financial analysts are opposed to the disclosure of current values, and most would welcome it. On the other hand, most analysts at this time are not prepared to abandon the historic-cost-based but eclectic system of valuation used in accounting today. In fact, many financial analysts are going to require much persuasion before they will be willing to accept expansion of the role of current value in financial statements themselves.

Much of the unwillingness of financial analysts to accept immediately a greater use of market values in financial statements stems from a perceived need for the utmost reliability in the numbers provided to them. They feel that even though historic costs are subject to certain manipulation, the situation could be worse with respect to numbers that are not verifiable by reference to a transaction in which the enterprise participated. Some analysts are concerned also about partial measures. They feel, for example, that marking the securities portfolio and (perhaps) other assets of a bank to market is misleading if that institution's liabilities are not revalued also. Their concern is the one expressed in the preceding section, that the financial report on the business will not reflect the manner in which it is managed.

The process of learning to understand and use new and unfamiliar financial information is longer and more arduous than one might expect. In Financial Accounting Standard No. 33 (FAS 33), we were provided with information that, although imprecise, was a godsend to those financial analysts who understood it and were able to use it in their work. Unfortunately, the five-year experiment by the Financial Accounting Standards Boards (FASB) came to an end before more than a modicum of financial analysts were able to take the necessary time from the press of their day-to-day duties to study and grasp the significance of inflation-adjusted data. That experience also was undermined by the incessant claims of individual business enterprises that the disclosures required by FAS 33 were worthless and by the rapid decline in the rate of inflation during that five-year period.

Our position is that we would like current value reporting to be given a chance.[2] We need to be able to assess the extent to which volatility really exists, even though the financial statements themselves may, as a political matter, need to be shielded from it. As long as current values are not seen, financial analysts cannot use them. The vehicle of disclosure, however, should be used so as to offer financial analysts the opportunity to use current values. They should not be coerced into it by a sudden and unilateral removal from financial statements of the historic costs and other amounts which are familiar and useful to so many analysts.

## Recognize All Executory Contracts

We all have struggled to understand the immense body of detailed rules that govern accounting for leases. Sometimes it seems as if the only persons having sufficient motivation to study their particulars are those who need to write lease contracts that produce desired outcomes. We know that the criteria for distinguishing between capital lease and operating lease set forth in Financial Accounting Standard No. 13 and its supplements are arbitrary and their application often is willfully capricious. Sometimes it seems as if the opportunities to manipulate the rules are in direct proportion to their copiousness.

We believe the rules could be simplified. First, we would drop the current dichotomy between accounting standards for leases and those for other executory contracts. We would have them treated the same way. Second, we believe that financial reporting would be improved considerably if all executory contracts of more than one year duration were capitalized. That would result in the recognition of all receivables and payables at the present value of future legally enforceable commitments to exchange cash in the

[2]To this end, a subcommittee of the FAPC is preparing a far-reaching study of opinions of AIMR members on the mark-to-market issue.

future. Our reasoning is set forth earlier in this report.

## Develop Standards for Reporting Comprehensive Income

Financial analysts continue to place heavy emphasis in their work on the income statement. It produces the numerator of earnings per share calculations and the denominator of the price-to-earnings ratio, two stalwart numbers in the investment world. Analysts also recognize that earnings comprises a multitude of components of varying quality: some are repetitive, others are not; some are operating items, others are not; some are the product of accounting rituals, others are not; some represent economic events of the current period, others do not. Much effort is required of analysts to locate and evaluate all of the income statement items that can have a bearing on their forecasts of the future and the valuation of the firm.

Much of this report is devoted to marshalling evidence and arguments to support our position that the FASB needs to move comprehensive income from concept to application. We believe the arguments are strong and hope to see progress in this matter in the not-too-distant future.

## Provide Frequent and Detailed Financial Reports

Interim financial reporting requirements in the United States have been the subject of much unjust criticism. They have been blamed for everything from "short termism" to a degradation in U.S. competitiveness. Not only are those charges without merit, they also fail to credit interim reporting for its vital role in keeping investors informed, diminishing opportunities for trading on privileged information, and maintaining peak efficiency of the financial markets. We believe we present in this report and elsewhere[3] valid reasons to continue mandated quarterly financial reporting.

One of the primary deficiencies in contemporary financial reports is the minuscule amount of disaggregated data. In annual reports, that which is provided usually is skimpy, and many firms have interpreted the provisions of Financial Accounting Standard No. 14 so as to report fewer segments than an analyst might expect, and segments sometimes are defined by the firm in peculiar ways. Not only are we in urgent need of new definitions and disclosure requirements to emanate from the FASB project on disaggregation, we also need segment reporting extended to interim reports. Analysis of a

---

[3]Korn, *op. cit.*

complex enterprise with diverse operations is futile in the absence of significant quantities of disaggregated financial data.

## Cost/Benefit Analysis from a User Viewpoint

The benefits of producing financial statement information should exceed the cost of producing it. That is an axiom often cited by financial statement preparers in opposing a proposed change in financial reporting practice. We not only do not object to that precept, we support it strongly. Our objection is to how it is portrayed by others.

We believe it is the owners of business firms who both reap the benefits and bear the costs of improvements in accounting and disclosure standards. The financial managers of business firms act simply as agents of the owners. In that regard, it is the current and potential shareholders and their financial advisors who should best be able to advise standard-setting and regulatory bodies as to the proper balance of costs and benefits associated with their proposals.

This position is corollary to the overall stance of AIMR, all other investors, and other users of financial statements. Financial statements are prepared and disseminated to provide the information that free financial markets need to operate. Users are the customers to be served. They also pay for the benefits they receive, albeit indirectly. Sometimes financial statement users are accused of being "free riders," receiving all of the benefits of financial reporting and paying none of the costs. The illogic and untruth of that statement must be apparent to anyone who makes the effort to analyze it thoughtfully. If not, then this report has failed to meet one of its goals.

# CONCLUSIONS

This report is the latest in a series of occasional position papers prepared by the Financial Accounting Policy Committee of AIMR. It is the first of those to undergo due process involving the AIMR Board of Governors and all of AIMR's constituent societies. It sets forth the position of investment advisors and financial analysts on the universe of financial reporting as it affects analysis today and into the next century. It explains in much detail the function of financial analysis, its sources and uses of information in general and in financial reports in particular. It speaks to trends that are expected to change practices both in analysis and accounting during the next decade or more. It addresses many issues of current importance and controversy. Some of its overall conclusions are mentioned below.

The interaction of financial analysis and financial reporting is one that increases enormously the level of efficiency in the capital markets. One of the major tenets of a free-enterprise economic system is that information is disseminated completely and fairly to all market participants. That is, of course, an ideal that in reality must be considered as an unattainable goal against which to measure actual achievement. Placed in that context, our positions in this report are eminently supportable despite the fact that in many cases they call for substantial expansion of the quantity and quality of financial information now being reported.

The role of the attest function receives somewhat less attention herein. We have observed much turmoil in the world of public accounting and are hard put to prognosticate its future course. We continue to consider attestation necessary to the credibility of financial reports but have suggestions as to how it can be made more effective and efficient. We suggest a longer view of the process at present with a shift of emphasis from transaction-based to systems-based auditing. The role of the external auditor might subtly shift from attestation to "reliability enhancement."

A major portent for changing the future of financial reporting is the fact that capital markets now are global. That has led to both conflict and promise. The downside is the view of certain prominent market officials that the current high level of accounting and disclosure standards that we enjoy in the United States be relaxed so that more foreign securities can be traded in U.S. markets. AIMR will continue to combat that movement with all of its resources.[1] The good news is that there are accelerating attempts to internationalize accounting

---

[1]See Appendix B for a list of comment letters from AIMR's SEC Liaison Committee to the SEC. Several of the letters deal with international security registration issues.

standards by the International Accounting Standards Committee together with an increased interest on the part of national standards-setting bodies to support that process.

Finally, we note the reasons why financial analysts and other financial statement users sometimes are viewed as outsiders or even nonparticipants in the standard-setting process. Financial reporting is not the focus or total *raison d'etre* of their employment. Unlike accounting professionals, financial analysts participate as volunteers and often to the detriment rather than enhancement of their professional development and standing. More importantly, financial analysts have infrequent opportunities to sit in the seats of decision-making power. Their comments are sought but sometimes either not heard or heeded. The view of them as outsiders stems less from their unwillingness or inability to participate than from their exclusion from the process. The FASB has had seven members throughout the 20 years of its existence, a total of 140 man-years. Five of those years (3.76 percent) were contributed by a financial analyst. Only as the board enters its third decade has a second practicing analyst been appointed as a member. Financial statement users need much more of a *direct* voice in the process than they have been given in the past.

Throughout the report, we make many other recommendations and establish positions on a variety of issues. Those matters are set forth for two purposes. First, they announce to the rest of the world our thoughts on issues of mutual importance to investment professionals and other constituents in the world of financial reporting. Second, they provide an opportunity for AIMR members to form their individual thoughts about the implications of financial reporting and its potential effect on their work in the 1990s and beyond.

# APPENDIX A
## FAPC COMMENT LETTERS,
## APRIL 8, 1988, through APRIL 6, 1993

| Date | Recipient | Subject Matter |
|------|-----------|----------------|
| April 8, 1988 (Revised May 24, 1988) | FASB | Proposed FAS "Disclosure About Financial Instruments" |
| May 10, 1988 | FASB | Proposed FAS "Disclosure About Financial Instruments" |
| July 15, 1988 | FASB | Proposed Technical Bulletin, "Definition of a Right of Set Off" |
| June 8, 1989 | SEC (Commissioner Ruder) | "Statement of Financial Analysts Federation on Summary Reporting" (a joint report of the FAPC and the SEC Liaison Committee) |
| August 7, 1989 | FASB | Proposed FAS "Employers' Accounting for Post-Retirement Benefits Other Than Pensions" |
| August 31, 1989 | SEC | Report to the FAPC of its subcommittee on quarterly segment reporting |
| September 29, 1989 | SEC | Proposed rules for increased auditor involvement with quarterly information |
| September 29, 1989 | FASB | Proposed FAS "Disclosure of Information About Financial Instruments with Off-Balance-Sheet Risk and Financial Instruments with Concentrations of Credit Risk" |
| September 29, 1989 | IASC | E33—Proposed "Accounting for Taxes on Income" |
| September 29, 1989 | FASB | Proposed FAS "Statement of Cash Flows—Net Reporting of Certain Cash Receipts and Cash Payments and Reclassification of Cash Flows from Hedging Transactions" |
| October 5, 1989 | IASC | E32—Proposed "Comparability of Financial Statements" |

| Date | Recipient | Subject Matter |
|------|-----------|----------------|
| December 28, 1989 | IASC | E34—Proposed "Disclosures in the Financial Statements of Banks and Similar Financial Institutions" |
| February 8, 1990 | Financial Accounting Foundation | Recommendations of the Financial Accounting Foundation Structure Committee on FASB voting procedures |
| May 7, 1990 | FASB | Restructuring country debt exposure; accounting and disclosure issues |
| May 7, 1990 | IASC | E35—Proposed "Financial Reporting of Interests in Joint Ventures" |
| June 15, 1990 | IASC | IASC Statement of Principles, "Financial Instruments" |
| July 25, 1990 | Accounting Standards Executive Committee of the AICPA | Proposed Statement of Position, "Reporting by Financial Institutions of Debt Securities Held as Assets" |
| July 25, 1990 | IASC | IASC Statement of Principles, "Cash Flow Statements" |
| October 31, 1990 | SEC (Commissioner Lochner) | Various accounting and disclosure issues |
| January 16, 1991 | FASB | Discussion memorandum related to "Distinguishing between Liability and Equity Instruments and Accounting for Instruments with Characteristics of Both" |
| April 8, 1991 | Financial Accounting Federation Oversight Board, (Michael Cook, Chairman) | Written comments on matters relating to the assessment of the FASB and its mission. |
| April 30, 1991 | FASB | Proposed FAS "Disclosures about Market Value of Financial Instruments" |

| Date | Recipient | Subject Matter |
|---|---|---|
| May 13, 1991 | SEC | Request for public comment of the acceptability in financial statements of an accounting standard permitting the return of a nonaccrual loan to accrual status after a partial charge-off |
| June 4, 1991 | FASB | Discussion memorandum related to "Present Value-Based Measurements in Accounting" |
| July 16, 1991 | FASB | Discussion memorandum related to "Accounting for the Impairment of Long-Lived Assets and Identifiable Intangibles" |
| September 6, 1991 | FASB | Proposed FAS "Accounting for Income Taxes" |
| November 7, 1991 | IASC | E38—Proposed "Inventories" |
| November 8, 1991 | IASC | E39—Proposed "Capitalization of Borrowing Costs" |
| January 20, 1992 | IASC | E36—Proposed "Cash Flow Statements" |
| April 1, 1992 | IASC | E37—Proposed "Research & Development Activities" |
| June 25, 1992 | FASB | Proposed FAS "Reporting by Defined Benefit Pension Plans of Investment Contracts" |
| June 25, 1992 | FASB | Proposed FAS "Accounting and Reporting for Reinsurance of Short-Duration and Long-Duration Contracts" |
| July 30, 1992 | FASB | Discussion memorandum related to "Recognition and Measurement of Financial Instruments" |
| July 30, 1992 | IASC | E40—Proposed "Financial Instruments" |
| August 28, 1992 | FASB | Proposed FAS "Recision of FASB Statement No. 32 and Technical Corrections" |
| August 28, 1992 | FASB | Proposed FAS "Employers' Accounting for Postemployment Benefits" |

| Date | Recipient | Subject Matter |
|------|-----------|----------------|
| September 16, 1992 | FASB | Discussion memorandum related to "Consolidation Policy and Procedures" |
| October 2, 1992 | IASC | E43—Proposed "Property, Plant and Equipment" |
| October 15, 1992 | FASB | Discussion memorandum related to "New Basis of Accounting" |
| October 19, 1992 | FASB | Proposed FAS "Accounting by Creditors for Impairment of a Loan" |
| December 9, 1992 | FASB | Proposed FAS "Accounting for Certain Investments in Debt and Equity Securities" |
| December 9, 1992 | IASC | E45—Proposed "Business Combinations" |
| December 18, 1992 | IASC | E41—Proposed "Revenue Recognition" |
| January 15, 1993 | FASB | Proposed FAS "Applicability of GAAP to Mutual Life Insurance Enterprises" |
| January 15, 1993 | IASC | E44—Proposed "Effects of Changes in Foreign Exchange Rates" |
| January 15, 1993 | IASC | E46—Proposed "Extraordinary Items, Fundamental Errors and Changes in Accounting Policies" |
| March 22, 1993 | IASC | E47—Proposed "Retirement Benefit Costs" |
| April 2, 1993 | FASB | Clarification letter regarding proposed FAS "Accounting by Creditors for Impairment of a Loan" |
| April 6, 1993 | FASB | Project on accounting for stock options |

# APPENDIX B
# OTHER COMMITTEE COMMENT LETTERS,
# FEBRUARY 2, 1989, through APRIL 10, 1993

| Date | Recipient | Sender | Subject Matter |
| --- | --- | --- | --- |
| February 2, 1989 | SEC | SEC Liaison Committee | Release No. 34-26390, File No. SR-NYSE-88-40, "Self-Regulatory Organization," proposed rule change by New York Stock Exchange, Inc., relating to the meaning, administration or enforcement of Rule 19c-4 |
| March 20, 1989 | SEC | SEC Liaison Committee | Release No. 33-6806, File No. S7-23-88, "Resales of Restricted Securities," changes to method of determining holding period of restricted securities under Rules 144 and 145 |
| April 19, 1989 | SEC | SEC Liaison Committee | Release No. 33-6821, File No. S7-6-89, "Securities Uniformity, Annual Conference on Uniformity of Securities Law." |
| June 30, 1989 | SEC | SEC Liaison Committee | File No. S7-7-89, regulatory flexibility agenda and rules scheduled for review |
| September 8, 1989 | SEC | SEC Liaison Committee | Release No. 33-6839, File No. S7-23-88, "Resale of Restricted Securities," International Series 104, changes to method of determining holding period of restricted securities under Rules 144 and 145 |
| September 29, 1989 | SEC | SEC Liaison Committee | Proposed rules for increased auditor involvement with quarterly information |
| November 6, 1989 | SEC | SEC Liaison Committee | Proposed rules for multijurisdictional disclosure |
| June 29, 1990 | SEC | SEC Liaison Committee | File No. S7-6-90, comments on anticipated rulemaking actions |

| Date | Recipient | Sender | Subject Matter |
|------|-----------|--------|----------------|
| October 1, 1990 | SEC | SEC Liaison Committee | Comments regarding multinational tender and exchange offers |
| December 14, 1990 | SEC | SEC Liaison Committee | Proposed rules for multijurisdictional disclosure (revised) |
| April 10, 1991 | SEC | SEC Liaison Committee | Release No. 33-6883, File No. S7-4-91, "Securities Uniformity, Annual Conference on Uniformity of Securities Laws" |
| May 10, 1991 | Accounting Standards Executive Committee of AICPA | AIMR Committee on Software Industry Financial Reporting Practices | Proposed statement of position on software revenue recognition |

# APPENDIX C
## FINANCIAL ACCOUNTING POLICY COMMITTEE
## JULY 14, 1992

Edward N. Antoian, CFA
  Delaware Management Company
  Philadelphia, Pennsylvania

John T. Ciesielski, Jr.
  R.J. Associates, Inc.
  Baltimore, Maryland
  (joined 1993)

Anthony T. Cope, CFA
  Wellington Management
  Company
  Boston, Massachusetts

Martin L. Flanagan, CFA
  Templeton, Galbraith &
  Hansberger, Ltd.
  Nassau, Bahamas

Peter H. Knutson, CPA
  The Wharton School
  University of Pennsylvania
  Philadelphia, Pennsylvania

Donald H. Korn, CFA
  DHK Associates, Inc.
  Boston, Massachusetts

Peter C. Lincoln
  U.S. Steel and Carnegie
  Pension Fund, Inc.
  New York, New York

Patricia A. McConnell, CPA
  Bear, Stearns & Company, Inc.
  New York, New York

Sharon M. McGarvey, CPA
  Metropolitan Life Insurance
  Company
  New York, New York

Milton L. Meigs, CFA
  Duff & Phelps, Inc.
  Chicago, Illinois

James M. Meyer, CFA
  Janney Montgomery Scott, Inc.
  Philadelphia, Pennsylvania

Christopher Rahne
  BDO Seidman
  New York, New York

Robert Renck, Jr.
  R.L. Renck & Company, Inc.
  New York, New York

Douglas Sherlock, CFA
  Sherlock Company
  Gwynedd, Pennsylvania

Paul Sloate
  Sloate, Weisman, Murray &
  Company
  New York, New York

Ashwinpaul C. Sondhi
  Columbia University
  New York, New York

William M. Stellenwerf
  Fitch Investor Service, Inc.
  New York, New York

Frances G. Stone, CFA
  Merrill, Lynch & Company
  New York, New York

Gerald I. White, CFA
  Grace & White, Inc.
  New York, New York